CONTAINER
and
RAISED BED GARDENING
for Beginners

2 books in 1

An Easy Guide to Grow Fresh Organic Vegetables

Hannah Roses

Table of Contents

CONTAINER GARDENING *for* *Beginners*

An Easy Guide to Grow Fresh Organic
Vegetables and Ornamental Plants
in Pots and Tiny Spaces

INTRODUCTION

Container gardening is a trendy new trend for people who may not have enough room for conventional gardening or want to grow plants in a smaller space such as a patio or balcony. There are a few simple things to learn before beginning a container garden.

Although any container can be used for container gardening, water should be able to leave to prevent plants from getting too much water at any time. Place a small hole in the jar to remove excess water. You can go to a gardening store for a simple choice of wooden, ceramic, or plastic garden pots. Many people enjoy using unique items from attics, antique shops, or even constructing their own. The sky is the limit, and you can easily design your container garden.

Use good-quality soil after selecting the correct container. Choose high-quality potting soil and select some fertilizer to help plants grow. Then choose where to put your garden. Sunlight is important since many plants require six or more hours of sunlight a day. Choose the best position for plant appearance and safety.

After gathering all supplies, pick your plants. For flowers year-round, start planting spring bulbs and then add summer plants in June or July. Daffodils, tulips, and hyacinths are perfect beauty options and hardy flowers. Some flower suggestions are iris, pansies, daisies, and crocuses. Choose your flowers based on the growing season. A perfect way to pick a color scheme is to look at flower catalogs and see what the bulbs are.

Growing plants in containers can be immensely rewarding and can be very therapeutic, like any planting. What could be better if you live in an apartment with a tiny balcony than watching your pot plant garden or picking some fresh herbs or vegetables grown in containers and using them in your cooking.

Package gardens benefit from being portable. If you move home, you can take your garden with you, or just want a change and rearrange your plants. In a very short time, your garden will look fresh. A container garden is not the flat one dimension of a traditional garden but gives you the additional height dimension. By using pots of different heights or putting them on tables, you will gain from several plant rates. It's nice to cover walls or untidy places. Your portable garden's design and look are limited by ingenuity and imagination.

Being able to raise your container garden off the ground and ease of maintenance means these gardens are suitable for the elderly or wheelchair users, where falling to ground level and using heavy garden tools are not a choice. This is one of the most important advantages of potting plants and demonstrates how flexible they can be.

CHAPTER ONE
The Best Potting Soil

If you are thinking of planting in your garden or creating your own garden for plants, it is more than likely that you want to know which soil is best for plant growth. The type of soil and the quality varies depending on where you are living, and even the soil in your garden does not have to be the same as that of your neighbor. The soil that is best for growing plants directly will be seen on the same plants that they grow.

Let's talk about outdoor and indoor soils so that you can see the differences between them, and you can decide for yourself the best soil for the growth of plants.

Floors outside

Outdoor floors are usually of three different types:

- Of sand.
- Of clay.
- Slime or silt.

The best soil for most plants is one that is rich in nutrients and sandy soil. If you think that your soil does not meet the suitable conditions because you can always modify its conditions and make them optimal with a little fertilizer.

Indoor floors

If you have plants that are growing indoors, you may think it is a good idea to get the soil out into the garden for your plants to grow there, but this is a common mistake and also a bad idea.

Garden soil contains bacteria that can kill your houseplants. There's another option if you don't want to use the potting soil they sell in stores: sterilize the soil outside.

Sterilize the exterior floor

If you choose to decide that your indoor plants grow outdoors, you will have to sterilize the soil outside to eliminate diseases and get rid of insects and weeds. After sterilizing the soil, you will have to modify the soil with peat and sand, so your plants will have adequate drainage and the correct air so that there is good humidity.

You can also choose to buy commercial potting soil because they are very similar and more comfortable for you. These soils include peat moss and vermiculite; something that will cause a slow release of fertilizers suitable for the growth of your plants.

Both aspects will help your plants grow with strong roots because they will be able to obtain nutrients, humidity, and adequate ventilation.

Know The Types Of Soil For Your Garden

To achieve a dream garden or have a well-kept corner of leafy plants, it is important that you know the types of soil, their characteristics, and knows which one you need for each plant. The quality of the land is important!

Choosing the right substrate is also important for our crops to look good. Each type of soil has its particular physical and chemical characteristics, and in the market, you can get several types, but that will depend on the particular needs of your plant.

A substrate can make your plants more resistant to pests and other elements that can hinder their growth, as well as protect them from parasitic diseases.

Would you like to learn what you have about the land for cultivation and which ones are better suited to your plant type? Everything you're reading below is going to be very useful.

1. Prepared land

It is the best substrate for pots because they have good water drainage. The prepared soil is the one used for the best growth of ornamental plants that you place in pots, planters, flower beds, and gardens.

The prepared soil is the one recommended for the moment of sowing a new plant in a pot; this way, you can be sure that its growth process will be optimal from the beginning.

This type of commercial land has a set of common components, among the most prominent of which are moss, compost, and rice husk.

2. Professional land

This type of soil helps moisture retention and activates natural plant protection systems. It contains significant percentages of nitrogen, an ideal element for growing plants. The professional soil also has a mixture of black peat, peat moss, granules, and perlite. When is it useful? Professional soil is suitable for any crop, both outdoors and indoors.

Among the benefits of using this substrate is the fact that thanks to its components, the plants will be healthier and stronger against diseases. Another advantage of professional soil is that it is ideal for the root development of plants, in addition to contributing to more regular and uniform growth because the stems will be more robust.

In summary, when you buy professional soil, your plants can count on a better metabolism and a low incidence of diseases. This will mean larger, stronger, and leafier plants.

3. Black Soil

Its origin was formed after the decomposition of organic matter, and it is suitable for pots and grasses. It is distinguished specifically by its color (dark black). Black earth is generally made up of remnants of dry leaves or organic waste of animals that are absorbed as nutrients by the soil.

This type of soil is beneficial when making a crop or planting plants. It is generally used for the sowing of ornamental plants or also for the cultivation of plants that serve for our subsequent feeding. Black soil plays an essential role in these crops because it contains the necessary nutrients that promote the growth of plants, fruits, or flowers.

There are many benefits of black earth, but we can mention its natural capacity to retain the water for the development of the plant. Also, its components are ideal for the circulation of the roots; in this way, the plant's growth is optimal and healthy.

4. Potting soil substrate

It is rich in nutrients and perfect for vegetables, foliage, and flowers. The substrate is one of the best for plants, given that it can grant fertility to the soil and provide the nutrients that the plant needs for its development to be as expected.

Among the types of substrates, we can mainly highlight two types: organic and inert substrates. Among the organic substrates, one of the most outstanding is earthworm humus, a type of substrate that provides greater fertility to the soil thanks to its particular composition: nitrogen, phosphorus, potassium, calcium, magnesium, iron, and sodium, among other elements.

Furthermore, this substrate can inhibit the development of fungi and bacteria that can affect plants. Another of the best-known organic substrates is mulch, a type of substrate responsible for preventing early erosion and provides a set of organic materials to the earth to protect it against high or low temperatures.

Coconut fiber, perlite, gravel, and sand are in the group of inert substrates. This set of substrates has the perfect components to nourish plants and allow good drainage of the soil and maintain the correct humidity for its development.

5. Leafy ground

Leafy soil improves its texture and allows better internal air passage. Leafy soil is considered the "black gold" of plants because it can provide a large number of nutrients.

You will notice its effects because your plants will be able to germinate better, their growth will be much faster, and their appearance will look stronger. By the time you decide to add leaf soil to your crops, you will be automatically improving the composition of the soil, as well as enriching it with various nutrients.

6. Organic land

Organic soil improves moisture retention and gives greater resistance to the plant. A great advantage is that it can be used on all types of plants. Organic soil is part of the fertilizer that should be given to plants in order to make their growth healthier.

Some expert gardeners use it as a garden filler because this type of soil has the ability to increase the number of nutrients in the soil.

7. Special lands

The special lands, due to their composition, are ideal for certain types of flowers, such as orchids. These soils have the ability to provide the nutrients that floral plants need to make them look beautiful, with leafy leaves and brightly colored flowers.

Do you already know what type of land to choose? Beautifying a garden is more than just planting some plants and adding water from time to time. If you want healthy and strong ornamental plants, you have to look where you walk; yes, the lands are essential to achieve that goal. The diet of a plant and the absorption of nutrients will depend on the quality of the land you have purchased, and currently, all you need to know is the plant you have in order to buy the right substrate.

Having a garden, land, plants, and flowers in excellent conditions is not impossible; it begins by choosing the right soil and the correct composition. Then everything will be easier: watch your little plant grow and grow stronger day by day.

If you are thinking of planting in your garden or creating your own garden for plants, it is more than likely that you want to know which soil is best for plant growth. The type of soil and the quality varies depending on where you are living, and even the soil in your garden does not have to be the same as that of your neighbor. The soil that is best for growing plants directly will be seen on the same plants that they grow.

CHAPTER TWO
Gardening Month By Month

In the greenhouse, the seasons punctuate the work from the vegetable garden to the orchard, going through the ornamental garden: the soil, like plants, needs rest periods until it flourishes again with spring's arrival.

From January to December, the garden work evolves every month with periods more intensive than others: tillage, sowing, seeding, planting, harvesting. Reminder sheets so that nothing can be missed or overlooked, and take good care of the fruits and vegetables that are grown. You'll also be exploring all the regular garden plays.

In the garden in January: what to plant, sow and do in January?

January is clearly not the most favorable outdoor gardening month: frosts, wind, fog, and snow are often breaks. Moreover, the vegetation is at rest; it takes time to start spring again!

It's time to think about the layout of your garden, though, by redesigning it; for instance, in front of your desk, warm in front of a fireplace, with hot chocolate and some small chocolate hazelnuts madeleines!

Vegetable gardening in January: preparing the soil, planting, and sowing

- The leek should be protected from excessive frost by a good layer of straw or leaves.
- Do good plowing, incorporating the manure previously deposited in your soil.
- You can plant garlic and shallot bulbs. Under heated chassis, you will sow carrots. Under shelter, you can sow spring lettuces.
- Prepare the trenches for planting asparagus in the spring.
- It's time to check your seeds' expiration dates and clean your pea or row bean stakes with iron sulfate or bleach.

Gardening in the ornamental garden and flower beds in January

- In the ornamental garden, some flowering plants give colorful touches: Christmas roses, heather, camellias. But, it will especially be necessary to prepare the garden for the end of winter. The Christmas party is over, and if you bought a Nordmann tree, for example, with roots, you need to replant it very quickly.
- First, plow the spaces that will receive annuals and claw the flowerbeds of biennials.

- Protect perennials from frost too intense with mulch, and clean by removing dried flowers and stems. Protect some shrubs that fear frost with a veil.
- Prepare the earthworks for your future lawn, if necessary. If you have a pool, break the ice that could have formed. Also, remember to feed small birds that suffer a little in winter!

In the garden in February: what to plant, sow and do in February?

February's weather is oddly close to January's, with the fact that the days get a little longer. It's common practice to say February is one of the coldest months.

It is indeed the full winter sports season because there's snow! And either you're staying warm at home, dreaming and planning what you're going to do in your garden in the months ahead, or you're quitting your garden for a couple of days and going to the ski slopes for sports sliding!

Gardening in the vegetable patch in February

- Harvest the leeks and Brussels sprouts.
- Sow in a greenhouse or frame carrots, summer leeks, and lettuces. Plant the pink garlic and the claws of asparagus in the trenches prepared in January.

- Clean your strawberry planks: dry leaves and weeds. Divide the rhubarb feet.

Figure 1- hydrangeas

Gardening in the ornamental garden and flower beds in February

Figure 2- Azalea

- Plant the biennials if you haven't finished. There is still time to divide and replant the perennials. Plant rhododendrons and azaleas. Make your chrysanthemum cuttings and start sowing flower seeds for the summer.

- Clean hydrangeas by cutting dry branches.

- Prune roses and prune shrubs or vines that bloom on year-round wood.

- Devote yourself to your lawn since there is little to do for the flowers: redraw its borders, air it, scarify it, sow it if you are at the creation stage!

- Take advantage of your first flowerings: crocuses, primroses, daffodils.

In the garden in March: what to plant, sow and do in March?

Figure 3- tomato seedling

March's rains are typical of this crucial month, with bursts of heavy rain, snow, slush, and sleet between the end of winter and the beginning of spring. So far, don't hurry to the greenhouse since relatively extreme colds can still occur: these March sleet only signal the spring's gradual arrival, so you can continue your greenhouse interventions more intensively.

The flowers are progressively growing, the winter defenses can be slowly eliminated, and according to the well-known adage, you will be able to indulge in the March sizes, considered the highest.

Gardening in the vegetable patch in March

- Seedlings of lettuce, chicory, broad beans, cabbage, spinach, turnips, parsnips, beets, radishes, celery, and peas can be started, just like the leeks that you will transplant at the end of June for a fall-winter harvest after.
- If you have a warm mini greenhouse, the first sowing of tomatoes can be made. Aromatics such as basil, parsley, mint, rosemary, thyme, and chives, will also be sown undercover.
- Potatoes can be planted after proper smoking.
- Also, pink plant garlic and white onion.

- If you have artichokes, take the most beautiful eyecups on the feet to transplant them and multiply the feet.

Gardening in the ornamental garden and flower beds in March

Seasonal flowers show up and start to brighten up the garden: primroses, serviceberry, Japanese quince, prunus, mimosa, and of course, the essential yellow forsythia heralding the arrival of spring!

- In the ornamental garden, remove and store the winter protections.
- Put compost at the foot of irises and peonies.
- Plant perennials as well as summer and fall flowering bulbs.
- Sow annuals, only under cover: petunias, verbena, sage, marigold, cosmos.
- For shrubs, prune all hedges and deflower camellia, hibiscus, buddleia, wisteria. Also, your last roses.
- Finish planting the deciduous bare-rooted shrubs and evergreen shrubs.
- Treat oleanders with Bordeaux mixture to avoid bacteriosis or pseudomonas, which manifests itself in black spots.

In the garden in April: what to plant, sow and do in April?

It's spring in April, but beware; the saying "Don't discover yourself by the thread in April" is still true! There is no hurry to expect too much sowing or planting at the risk of a late frost wiping out your efforts.

The world is slowly heating up, leaves and flower buds are bursting, but maintain defenses on the most vulnerable plant species as a precaution. Nothing is won yet, particularly since the reddish moon is conducive to night frosts during the lunation after Easter that makes young shoots russet.

Gardening in the vegetable patch in April

- Planting of melons, squash, carrots, cabbage, spinach, green beans, radishes, lettuce, beets, and other vegetables can begin.
- Plant early potatoes and leeks in summer, along with rave celery and ribbed celery.
- You will need to thin the carrot seedlings made in March, leaving a plant every 4 to 5 cm.
- It's time to transplant lettuce plants.
- Divide the chives, sow the parsley.

- Prepare the earth where you will plant your tomatoes. Only regions with a mild climate will be able to start planting them during the second half of April.

The ornamental garden in April: flower beds, trees, and shrubs

Spring is here with the blooming of all the bulbs hidden in the beds, lawns and tubs of terraces: tulips, hyacinths, daffodils, and muscaris. Perennial side, the silver basket is in bloom, like the asters and the heart of Mary. The periwinkles, the thoughts are resplendent, and the lilac scents. It is also the month of the syringe, the magnolia, the ceanothes, the azalea, the rhododendron, and the orange tree of Mexico.

- Sow the annual flowers directly in place: forecastle, California poppy, nasturtium, snapdragon, cosmos, and zinnia.
- Plant perennials in your beds.
- Plant the dahlias and the bulbs that will bloom in summer or fall (lilies, gladioli, cannas ...).
- It's time to prepare the balconies and terraces planters that you will garnish with summer flowers.
- Repot the oleanders in containers, which need them.
- As time goes by, remove the wilted flowers from the daffodils, hyacinths and tulips without touching the leaves or bulbs.

- There is no emergency going to buy your summer flowers in a garden center, even if it is tempting!
- Prune the spring flowering shrubs at the end of it.
- Cut the hydrangeas and lay the wisteria.
- Plant conifers, as well as shrubs and roses in containers. Hoe at the foot and mulch them.
- Make your first hedge pruning.

Other small interventions in April

- At home, repot your green plants, which are a bit cramped.
- Make the first mowing of the grass and scarify if necessary.

In the garden in May: what to plant, sow and do in May?

In May, valley lily opens the month with the May 1st tradition! It's the peak of spring: all the plants burst and expand noticeably with the wonderful days. A tiny field; look out for the Ice Saints: a late jelly can be fatal for some plants or for some shrubs!

The flowers give color and fragrance symphony: anemones, imperial fritillaries, columbines, bellflowers, Mary's heart, iris, lupins, peonies ... Without overlooking the flowering of shrubs such as laburnum, ceanothe, deutzia, magnolia, tamarisk, Judas vine, and much more, including the famous and beautiful lilac!

Gardening in the vegetable patch in May: planting, sowing, harvesting

- Sowing in the open ground of chives, carrots, turnips, fennel, pumpkins, parsley, lettuce, beans, tetragon can be undertaken,
- The cauliflower and autumn cabbage will be transplanted,
- The feet of tomatoes can be placed everywhere in the ground, as well as eggplants, melons, peppers, and basil,
- The radish and asparagus harvest is at its maximum. Do not forget to sow radishes every ten days to have a staggered harvest,
- Harvest the salads,
- The chicory seedlings that will make your endives next winter are to be done now.

The ornamental garden in May: flower beds, trees and shrubs

- All summer flowers can now be placed in the ground (or in planters), including geraniums,
- You can still do annual sowing in place, including climbers (nasturtium, bohemian, sweet pea),

- Plant lilies of the valley in the shade,
- If you have a pond, you can plant water lilies and pond plants there
- Cut the stems of perennials that are deflowered (iris, aubrietes…) without touching the leaves,
- Crop roses, remove gourmets of roses, suckers of lilac and hazelnut,
- Tear off the deflowered spring bulbs and continue planting the summer bulbs,
- Take out the cacti and succulents as well as the plants in the tub (oleander …).
- Prune spring-flowering shrubs as well as coniferous hedges,
- Plant ornamental shrubs bought in containers,
- Prune the heather that has finished flowering,
- Make hydrangea cuttings!

Other small interventions in May

- At home, during the second half of the month, gradually bring out the plants which are hardy enough to spend the summer outside on the terrace,
- If you have a veranda or a greenhouse, ventilate it well during the day,
- Lawn mowing should now be weekly,
- Watch for powdery mildew, aphids, slugs, rust, etc.

- Do your maintenance work on floors, fences, low walls, and underground watering.

In the garden in June: what to plant, sow and do in June?

"In June, if it rains, feed your fist" Oh? Funny comment, but what of a prologue! Fortunately, the saying library seems to find a great source of inspiration in June, and something more inspiring must be included ... "Beautiful sunshine that comes in June has never ruined anybody." That's better, and what could be more true?

June is the month with all dreams, marking the end of spring and the beginning of summer. The sun begins becoming a frequent resident; the first tanning marks emerge, indicating long lazing sessions on the beach. But we're not there yet (a little abrupt back to reality, but let's not hide anything; all these beautiful images are there only for the poetic side). Let's then go back to our goats. Holiday time hasn't come yet, much less for the gardener who won't get bored in the coming month.

The vegetable garden in June

Weeding, hoeing, watering. There will be no shortage of activities this month in the vegetable patch. No matter what happens, weeding and hoeing are essential so that weeds do not encroach on the vital space of your vegetables.

Of course, watering will depend more on the season and on the plant. If the weather is not too dry, settle for a punctual watering, preferably in the evening. Seedlings must, however, benefit from daily watering to get up well (again, they prefer to water in the evening so that all the water does not evaporate).

Other activities are also required during June for many vegetables:

- Butter: peas, beans, potatoes (already start to prevent the risk of downy mildew)
- Prune: tomatoes, melons
- Stake: cucumbers, pickles
- Lighten: carrots, lettuce, beets, turnips
- Sow: Brussels sprouts, autumn cauliflower, chard, squash
- Transplant: leeks,
- Harvest: garlic, shallots, onions, early potatoes, spinach, carrots

In addition to seasonal activity, we must also think about the future and start preparing for the next harvest by sowing certain vegetable plants. You can also sow strawberries for future seasons.

The ornamental garden in June

The ornamental garden also generates its share of activities. Sow the last annuals in the beds. Butte, the gladioli, mulch the dahlias, and plant the fall bulbs (Naples cyclamen, crocuses, crocus...). Sow poppies in the field and hollyhocks in the nursery.

Remember to regularly remove faded flowers to avoid the rise in seeds and to promote flowering.

For the cuttings, divide the spring perennials after flowering: delphinium, lupine, népéta...

Weed the beds, water, and mulch, and then mow the lawn regularly!

In the garden in July: what to plant, sow and do in July?

"Everyone who sleeps until the rising sun in July will inevitably die late" ... And the proverb is true. The month of July marks the beginning of the summer, the holidays, and the long relaxing hours in the pool hammock. But as jovial and fun as they may be, all these things should not make you forget the life of your vegetable garden, which will inevitably perish if you abandon it on such a good road.

July is the month of performance, and it is during this period, that the fruit of your efforts begins to become truly concrete! No major work in July, but a multitude of small "household" tasks to keep your garden balanced.

The vegetable garden in July

IN July, the vegetable garden is an authentic Spanish inn. All kinds of vegetables coexist; some depart, some arrive, and some are on the way. Therefore, this month will be the month of repairs, and we're going to have to handle this whole little universe and make sure everybody has everything they need. Daily hoeing is needed for most of them because the weeds that landed in the garden since June are not ready to decamp without a little hoe in the back. You should also remember to water regularly, preferably at night, to prevent the water from evaporating and not wet the leaves to prevent disease. Also, scrape the surface to crack the crust to make it easier for the water to penetrate.

- Butter: potatoes, beans (as soon as the first leaves are well developed).
- Prune: cucumbers, zucchini, tomatoes.
- Sowing: carrots and radishes (always sowing every two weeks for a regular harvest), lettuces, cabbage, turnips.
- Also, take advantage of an empty garden plot to sow your green manure.

The ornamental garden in July

The ornamental garden is probably the most affected part of your yard, as the flowers can't bear the heat well. Who has never returned from holidays to discover a mass of completely desiccated plants with dread? Therefore, you must help your flowers survive the stormy heat suffocating them by regularly watering in July (watering is not required every day either). Start by cleaning your beds and hoeing, and weeding your soil, so the water penetrates well. Again, watering in the evening is easier, but also monitoring the forecast to make sure it doesn't rain the next day. The plants are thirsty, but that isn't an excuse to drown them.

The time has come to tutor your dahlias and your gladioli to help them not to bow under the force of the stormy winds of July. If you go on vacation, remember to cut all the flowers of your roses and other flowering shrubs to benefit from a new flowering on the return.

For many plants, July is the month of multiplication:

- Cuttings: hydrangeas
- Tuft division: primroses and irises
- Harvesting of seeds: wallflowers, lupins, columbines, and poppies
- Harvest of spring bulbs

In the garden in August: what to plant, sow and do in August?

"Even though you like the diaper, don't sleep under the light of August." These words are really wise. Indeed, it's hardly advised to indulge in a nap under the hot rays of August unless you want to obey some fashion calling to go red from head to toe. And this heat is what drives most citizens to go on holiday this month. Just here, if you're happy to go far away and forget about work and trouble, the garden remains there and continues to claim its regular maintenance.

The vegetable garden in August

As with gardening in July, the garden is often full in August, and there is no shortage of work. Most vegetables are at the end of their growth and are preparing to leave the vegetable garden, so you have to watch out for the "final adjustments," which could hinder the final maturation phase. They will do very well if you've brought green manures to high-yielding vegetables, such as beans orchard, which tend to rob the soil of its nutrients.

- Transplant: seedlings from the previous month such as leeks, lettuce, cabbage.
- Sow: winter or late vegetables such as carrots, radishes, turnips, or lamb's lettuce.
- Harvest: the potatoes that must be left to dry before returning them.

- Multiply: division of rhubarb tufts by cutting them off using a tool like a spade.

The ornamental garden in August

The ornamental garden requires a lot of work in August. Some plants such as hollyhocks, amaranths, dahlias, and gladioli grow and are more fragile in the wind, so they must be staked.

It is also necessary to prune wilted flowers such as daylilies, cosmos, and lupins.

Transplant the biennials, like the wallflowers, which have reached a satisfactory size, transplant preferably in the evening. It will be necessary to water a little more abundantly than usual for a few days.

Continue to water regularly if the weather is too dry so that the plants do not wilt. If you go on a trip, abundantly water the base of your plants so that they have a good supply of water.

If you want to dry some of your flowers (hydrangeas, for example), it's time to pick them and hang them upside down in your basement or cellar.

Finally, make sure that ants and aphids do not invade the territory.

In the garden in September: what to plant, sow and do in September?

"Buy wood and clothes in September!" While the weather is still mild and sunny, winter is not far away, and we'll have to start preparing ourselves for the cold December and other months of not-so-warm temperatures at home and in the garden! Of course, without forgetting (to start in the good news), that September is the month of the school year's starting. No more hours of sun rest and early nap on the terrace lunch. Give way to screaming alarm clocks at midnight, hours lost in traffic congestion, and dishes with a more than dubious presence in the canteen.

The vegetable garden in September

The vegetable garden likes the September month (obviously, it is not he who comes back to work the guy!). The soil is perfect, though retaining last summer's heat; it also finds the autumn nights' humidity that gives the garden's soil a real renewal. September brings the end of summer with it, and at the end of the season, the gardener will have to enjoy his last tomatoes and other vegetables while a great maintenance job awaits him.

- Transplant: curly chicory and escarole under a forcing veil
- Sow: lamb's lettuce, chervil, onions, spinach, leeks, and radishes. Also, sow parsley in pots for the winter.

- Plant: strawberries! This September is a small ray of sunshine; strawberries love this end of season's warm and humid soil.
- Harvest: all the root vegetables, the potatoes (continuing to let them dry on the spot before bringing them in), the rhubarb petioles, and the last tomatoes that you can let ripen in the sun.

The ornamental garden in September

The ornamental garden shows itself to be much less sympathetic and loads you with its lot of work. As for the previous month, you must regularly remove the faded flowers from your beds, especially dahlias, to obtain future vigorous flowers.

Fold down the flower stalks of hollyhocks and give all the roses organic fertilizer.

It is now time to plant the bulbs collected last spring. The daffodil bulbs must be loosened every other year.

Also, sow poppies (to get flowers next spring) and chrysanthemums.

Transplant the biennials that have reached a satisfactory size.

There is still time to cut roses, fuchsias, and geraniums for those who did not have time to go about it in August. Divide tufts of peonies.

Harvest the seeds of nasturtiums, marigolds, carnations, lupins, and moths. Before enclosing the seeds in a container (preferably opaque), allow them to air dry to prevent moisture from causing them to rot.

In the garden in October: what to plant, sow and do in October?

Indeed, the gardener will still not be able to rest on the garden side this month. It might just as well be a concession for those who were always hoping for a potential time-out: this would never happen. Under the Elbow, the garden will still have an occupation to confuse you. Yet, essentially, admit it, you like it. What would the gardener have been without a small hoe corner, a repot plant, or a prune tree? It's to prevent such a sense of uselessness that the October month gives him his share of the toil. This work will consist mainly of the last harvests and field preparation for the cold season.

The vegetable garden in October

During this time, life in the vegetable garden was relatively calm, and the plots were slowly cleared. It's time to get the vegetables harvested and stored in a dry place to protect them. Take your vegetables in the morning to keep them from rotting from the moisture, then let them dry all day. Among other items, the last pumpkins can be harvested with delicacy (shocks threaten to hurt them), then placed on a straw pad. Store the carrots, turnips, beets, and black radishes at the end of the month. Store them between two layers of sand in the night.

Sowing black radishes are always possible, but they will have to be placed under a frame so that they do not die of cold.

You can also plant garlic and shallots.

Celery must be tied to make it blanch.

The onions from early August must be transplanted.

The ornamental garden in October

Just as the ornamental garden is the one that suffers the most from the heat, it is also the one that suffers the most from harsh winters. So we will have to prepare all these little people so that they can survive without too much trouble.

This involves taking in overly chilly plants such as orchids, hibiscus, and most green plants.

Geraniums and oleanders should be placed in a cool, well-ventilated area. Take the opportunity to cut them to 10cm.

Also, bring in citrus fruits.

Remove the annual plants that are wilting, and cut the flower stalks of the hollyhocks and the wilted flowers of the crocosmias.

The dahlias are fragile and could bend under the slightly more violent autumn winds. It is, therefore, more prudent to tutor them.

You can now plant the spring bulbs in-depth, covering them with a protective layer, like peat.

Divide and replant perennials, as well as roses. Mulch the soil to protect the roots.

In the garden in November: what to plant, sow and do in November?

November is a rainy month: the late fall rain but not drier in winter. You'll harvest your last crops and start growing frost-fearing plants. It is mainly the time to plant your trees and shrubs because, as a popular saying goes, "At Sainte Catherine, all wood takes root!."

The vegetable garden in November

Harvest the last root vegetables and pick the Brussels sprouts. Protect the winter cabbage and butte the artichokes so that you can mulch more to protect them from frost.

Drain the garden hoses, especially those that are buried, and reinsert them. Disinfect all guardians before returning them.

Iit's time to clean the windows of your greenhouse.

Empty your compost bin so you can put new leaves in it.

The ornamental garden in November

Cleaning the beds is essential for perennials: remove all dry flowers and stems. Regarding chrysanthemums, do the same at the end of the month.

Divide the feet of some perennials and replant them immediately.

Plant the gladioli, dahlias, and cannas, and let them dry in the dry before storing them undercover.

Plant biennials and spring-flowering bulbs. Plant camellias and roses. Prune summer or fall flowering shrubs.

Early in the month, it's time to mow the lawn. Then clean, sharpen, and wipe your mower's blade, which you will store until the following year. Finally, regularly rake the leaves fallen on your lawn.

If you have a pond, remove the fallen leaves from it to prevent them from rotting, or protect your pond with a tarpaulin.

In the garden in December: what to plant, sow and do in December?

While December is not very favorable for the garden, some tasks can still be carried out. For starters, planting a few trees and shrubs would be possible, and growing a certain number of vegetables such as cabbage, or even applying a ground fertilizer to your soils, if they are not frozen.

Flowers

- Plant your new roses
- Weed and properly clean your flower beds

Vegetables

- Pull out dead annuals and biennials
- Harvest beets, carrots, cabbage, leeks, salsify ...

Fruits

- Plant your fruit trees
- Prune and prune if necessary

Trees and shrubs

- Plant your ornamental trees and shrubs
- Compost the last leaves, clean

- Remove the moss from the trees with a brush and/or brush them with lime

General maintenance

- Cover your surfaces if the ground is not frozen

Amend if necessary

CHAPTER THREE
The Right Pot for Every Plant

Far from being a secondary aspect, they are a crucial element for the development of a plant. Something that forces us to know a little more in-depth about the types of pots that exist and what are their different applications. The way to get it right when we choose it; and make our plant not only look prettier than it is, but above all, grow with health and well-being.

A pot or planter is not just the container in which we have a plant. It is also their home and their natural way of life. There are two compelling reasons why, beyond aesthetic questions, we choose a pot according to a plant's specific needs.

Types Of Pots: Interior Or Exterior?

At first glance, we can believe that a pot is still a pot and that it is perfect for any space. However, the types of indoor and outdoor pots vary substantially in the same way that the specific requirements of plants vary from one environment to another. For starters, if we have to choose pots for outdoor plants, we will have to consider some fundamental needs:

- Choosing a pot with the guarantee of correct drainage: especially for pots located in gardens or terraces and without a roof that covers them, it is essential to carefully review this topic. Keep in mind that in the pots exposed to rain, we cannot control the amount of watering, so being able to evacuate any excess is vital to prevent the roots of the plant from rotting. Sometimes the drainage holes are marked in the pot so that we can make them according to the use we are going to give them.

The clay pots allow the perspiration and evaporation of the water.

- Choosing a material resistant to frost and UV rays from the sun: reviewing this aspect will guarantee that the pots will maintain their original state and function in moments of extreme temperature, both upward and downward! In this last aspect, both fiberglass and plastic are ideal. We will always have to avoid metal and glass pots, which can break with changes in temperature.

- Choose pots that facilitate transportation: if we contemplate large plants in our garden or terrace, such as palm trees or fruit trees, we will have to choose pots that allow us to attach wheels to be able to move them easily.

When choosing between the types of pots when it comes to indoor plants, we will have fewer demands:

- Any material is suitable for indoor pots, including both glass and metal since the temperatures inside a house are always more stable and balanced.
- Opting for these types of pots will allow us to save up to 40% of water.

Opt for self-watering pots: a perfect option for indoor plants maintenance and minimizing cleaning around them. This type of pot has a specific tank for water, which will facilitate the irrigation work for plants that live in environments where there is environmental dryness.

Types Of Pots Specific To Some Plants

Besides knowing the final location of a plant before choosing between the various types of pots, telling us if you have particular needs is also important. Furthermore, there are plants that demand different pots, either by arranging their roots or by their needs for growth. When purchasing plants, this is something that never hurts to learn in order to give the plant just what it wants.

And while the aim is to find out about each plant, let's know some that will need special pots:

Bonsai pots

Since we all know that growing a bonsai is an art, the focus is not only on the plant's main product in this case but also on the environment that makes the central thing look even better. You should know pot is not just a bonsai frame; it's part of the whole thing.

Figure 4 - Bonsai

There are several types of pots with bonsai. The most popular are ceramic bonsai pots and mica bonsai pots, which can be found in various shapes: rectangular, oval, rounded, octagonal, dished, and probably the best-looking separate pot of water. The best pots are all made by hand and made according to ancient Chinese norms. You should also be aware that the color of the leaves changes when choosing the right color for your pot, making the visual connection between pot and tree.

So, what looks good may not look appealing in the winter months. The regular width or diameter of a pot should be close to the area the branches take. This does not apply entirely to pots on water-land where pots should be wider. Water-land pots are the rarest but potentially the best-looking dishes. These pots are split in the center and filled with soil on one side and water on the other.

Because of their shallow root systems, tray-type pots are ideal for both bonsai care and small cacti. The ideal container so that the roots of both of them can grow in width as they need.

Pots for succulent plants

It doesn't sound like much, but choosing the right pot to grow succulents is of utmost importance. You can greatly facilitate the care of these beautiful plants.

Succulent plants generally referred to as succulents, derive their name from the thickness and fleshiness of their base, leaves and roots. This particularity is due to the unique type of fabric that composes them, the aquifer parenchyma, which has the capacity to absorb the little water available in the regions of origin. It acts as a reservoir and releases water when needed during long periods of drought, typical of arid and dry places where succulents have adapted to live.

There are thousands of species, divided into various botanical families, in form, scale and colors, but all very original and exotic, varying much from one another. Even the shape has been determined for survival in nature, and in fact, these plants take on the strangest square, oval, and rosette shapes, and the proportions are usually reduced to a minimum to minimize respiration and suddenness. Some species have turned the leaves into thorns, conferring chlorophyll function on the plant.

- *Points to consider when choosing succulent pots*

The right pot can highlight the natural beauty of any succulent; even so, never buy a pot just for being beautiful.

First, make sure the pot has drainage holes. If they do not have them, the pot will retain the water, and the plant will rot.

On the other hand, some pots have holes, but they are small. When growing succulents, look for pots with the largest holes.

Prevent the substrate from being lost through the drainage using a maya that allows water to pass through but retains the soil.

Second, choose a pot that is slightly larger than the succulents. If the container is too large, it will retain too much water, and the plant will die.

- *What are the best succulent pots*

Every succulent collector really enjoys buying pots. There are countless options for colors, textures, patterns, shapes, and sizes on the market. Let's talk a little bit about the types of succulent pots on the market.

1. Clay pots

The best option for beginners in the world of succulents is clay pots. Clay or clay pots are made from raw soil and have many benefits for plants.

They are air permeable. That means that the soil and roots can breathe. This will be healthier for the plant if it remains in an environment where it does not receive much airflow.

Another advantage is that clay pots remove excess moisture. I guess its biggest downside is that they are easy to break if they fall off.

2. Ceramic flower pots

Ceramic flower pots have the same benefits as clay flower pots. The problem with many is that they don't have drainage holes.

Bottom holes can be drilled with a drill and glass drill. The process requires patience and practice.

Another option is to leave the succulent in the propagation pot and place it in a slightly larger second ceramic pot. When you water your plants, it will be necessary to remove them from the ceramic container.

3. Concrete pots

The pot's concrete is modern and clean. They are an excellent choice for succulent plants. Like ceramic pots, many sell them without a drain hole.

4. Plastic flower pots

Succulents can be grown in plastic pots with no problem. Of course, you must be very careful with irrigation because they tend to retain moisture.

The best thing about plastic pots is how colorful they are and how many options are on the market. Another benefit is that they are lightweight.

One downside is that the plastic pots are roasted in the sun. Be sure to buy thick pots. These will last longer.

5. Wooden flower pots

Wooden flower pots are becoming more and more fashionable. It gives a rustic style to any arrangement with succulents.

Wood pots work very well because it keeps the soil cool when the succulents are placed in the sun. What I don't know is how long these pots will last exposed to the elements before they rot.

6. Glass pots or terrariums

Despite the fact that succulents look beautiful in glass containers, I do not recommend their use.

Glass is waterproof. This will create evaporation and drainage problems. It is impossible to grow succulents in glass, but you have to be very careful with watering and where the arrangement is placed.

- *How to find the right size*

The most common mistake when growing succulents is planting them in pots too big for the size of the plant. Just pick pots a few inches wider than the succulent's circumference.

Suppose you have a succulent that is 3 centimeters wide. In this case, choose a pot with a diameter of 5 to 6 centimeters.

- *How to choose pots for succulents most suitable*

In choosing the most suitable succulent plant pots, it is necessary to consider the size of the plant and the type of roots; only the multiple and tangled ones adapt to each pot, but more often than not, it is advisable to choose a rather tall pot, and also considering the layer drainage that must be created on the bottom.

The pot should not be too small, even if the succulent plants tolerate them more than others; nor too large, because this means more land and, therefore, more water retained. Succulents fear above all, excess humidity. Therefore the most suitable material for pots for succulents is the earthenware, which, as mentioned, allows the soil to breathe. It is also possible to use a saucer in which to place sand or earth to be wet instead of soil, so that the pot absorbs the little moisture from the substrate and transmits it to the plant therefore, in a constant way.

Plastic pots are generally not suitable for succulents, especially black ones, given that they retain heat and transmit it to the plant, which can favor parasites and fungi.

CHAPTER FOUR
Recycled Pots

Anything that is made from recycled materials is welcome in The Green Blog, and that is why we are going to show you next, some nice recycled pots for the garden and with which you can plant all kinds of plants in addition to having your own fully decorated garden.

Recycled pots allow us to find an application for articles we may have thrown at home that is unhelpful. It is possible to fill the balconies, gardens or patios with color and originality from the pots that can be made from items like a bottle of wine, milk cartons and even old CDs or floppy disks that are no longer used.

All the materials that you will see below, not only do we surely have them at home, but they are also easily cleaned, and we can handle them without problems.

When it comes to making flower pots with recycled material, there are as many ways to do it as you can think of ideas. In the end, it's about looking at that container you were going to throw away, letting the light bulb light up, and by the time you want to realize it, you already have something new and original.

Of course, always be careful with the tools and materials used so that they are not dangerous or cause accidents.

Recycled flowerpots with plastic bottles, cans, and pallets, but surely once you get into them, you can think of many more ways to make your own designs.

Original Garden Pots

If we were to tell you about the best materials for the manufacture of recycled pots, then the metal will definitely be the leader of our ranking, and we could get it from soda cans. If you choose preserves to make pots, remember to put a thick plastic inside so that the water doesn't oxidize it.

Plastic is also a perfect material for making recycled pots, and it must also be said to be cheaper but more "hard" when handling items such as containers or bottles.

Glass is another recommended item to make your pots recycled for the garden, but it's more complicated than it is because we have to make holes to drain the plant. We'll need a thread soaked in alcohol and a glass drill bit if we want to make them. In general, glass is used as a container with plants growing in water, such as a pot.

Tretrapac boxes are also recycled materials that can be used for our pots. They work well, clean quickly and do not require additional elements.

As far as "unconventional" materials and objects are concerned, we can always take advantage of computer parts, toys, kitchen containers, and even new shoes.

We can already begin to see what kind of materials we have at home and make our recycled pots! Remember, it's a good idea to use apple cider vinegar to clean them.

Flower Pots With Plastic Bottles

As we can see, people's creativity is boundless and can concentrate on reuse items that allow for a reduction in waste production and environmental protection. We stated earlier that plastic is material for recycled pots. The plastic bottles can be quickly obtained and turned into a pot quite quickly.

Others have even made big plastic bottles of gardens. The positive thing is that we can create or even manufacture hanging pots in different sizes and shapes. In the picture below, you can find an example of a garden with the most convenient plastic bottles. You can find the following.

Flower Pots With Glass Bottles

The bottles can be recycled and made in various varieties. Many pots made of plastic bottles have already been seen, but you can do real wonders by using glass bottles. If not, check out this beautiful oval floral pot made of glass bottles. The truth is, this pot looks like a true professionals' job already and can be found in a small square in a neighborhood. The question is: How many bottles does the pot manufacturer have to use (nearly 300, I say)?

You also have far simpler possibilities to turn a glass bottle into a pot if you do not want to go into a "run" of the previous caliber. Again, there is no brand we want to endorse, but it's as easy as using a soda bottle.

You do not need to use bottles. Usually, you can turn any glass container in your house into pots. For example, typical preserves or jam jars are very common.

Pots With Yogurt Containers

Because we are talking about pots that are recycled, the Yogurt jar you have completed can also be used. Don't just throw them down! Don't throw them away! They can serve as a flowerpot when they are big.

Our idea is to convert the liter Yogurt containers into pots, using spray paints or applying templates to beautify your creation. Let the varnish or embroidery you have made dry; fill them with dirt and voila! You can use them, for example, for small spices to always have on hand in the kitchen.

Flower Pots With Books

This other idea is very original, and if you love books, which are really beautiful objects, their use is really fascinating. Obviously, you should have some fat books that you do not want to turn into a flower pot and then place it on a piece of furniture, perhaps on your desk or on your nightstand. It could also be a great gift idea!

To create this beautiful pot, you must cut a sufficient number of pages to insert, for example, a small fat plant (perfect for this type of container because it requires little care and especially little water). Next, place a plastic sheet around the space cut to prevent water and dirt from ruining the rest of the book.

Flower Pot With A Wooden Box

Making a flower pot with a wooden box is a simple procedure that provides a significant and natural product. With their impressive size, these containers can hold more than one floor: what would you use to transform your courtyard into a small plant garden, where fresh crops and spices are planted, or even a certain amount of salads are planted, or to produce colorful floral work on a patio or garden?

The wooden boxes are perfect for growing plants, and you only need a few tips: hand primer specifically to protect the wood from the sun and rain and ensure that water can flow underneath by a small opening, if not present, to prevent stagnation inside the pot.

Flower Pots With Concrete Or Cement

Cement pots are very trendy and original. However, all of us can produce an exquisite and very natural outcome. Use old food containers in plastic or carton, like molds, to give your designs the most diverse forms; a mix of one piece of cement and four parts of sand are enough.

Fill a jar with the mix, leave a hole and allow to dry for a few days. Eventually, you should have some holes in the drainage boiler. Next, you fill the earth, and voila in the vacuum! You can begin putting your plants now.

Flower Pots With Pallets

If you have a small terrace and used up space on the street, it's time to think about rising upwards. Nothing like wagering on the most famous recycled pots of all for this. The pallet planters with which you can cultivate several varieties of plants without having to occupy huge sizes.

Fix the pallet if it is broken and add a wooden panel corresponding to the part that rests on the wall; then choose the quality of the plants, which can be flowering plants or some vegetable varieties like cucumber or peppers position them in the platform's natural holes. If you opt for waterfall-growing plants, the effect will be very good, the pallet will hardly be noticed and you will get a real green wall.

Pots With Coffee Bags

If you are not a big fan of traditional flower pots, these recycled flower pots are ideal for you. We suggest that you make pots with jute bags, among which those of coffee or rice are perfect; you will get really original and absolutely cheap pots. Also, you will bet for care to the environment as these bags are made from materials completely recycled and biodegradable.

To accomplish that, you just have to fill your sacks with some soil and plant your flowers or aromatic herbs or even fat seedlings; these creations give your terrace a natural feel or wherever you want to put them.

Flower Pots With Cans

If you have creative skills, by painting old cans with paint, you can choose to make your own recycled pots, which are great because they have a smooth surface. You can draw what you want, adding rhinestones or beads with soft or vivid colors; there is no limit to the imagination!

It is also possible to stick colored or pre-printed fabrics around the jars or use the newspapers we saw before; the only precaution during construction is to drill the drainage holes before adding soil and seedlings.

More Recycled Garden Pots

Some are looking for other more original and fun solutions. For example, do you remember those wellies (or katiuskas) that you used to wear and that you never wear anymore because they are too small for you or you have moved to an area where they are not necessary? Well, you can also turn your wellies into fun garden pots. You could even paint them as data to make them even more beautiful.

Following clothing, others decide to turn their pants into garden pots. The truth is that they give a slightly strange impression, but it is a good way to reuse clothes that we no longer use.

Toy Animals

How often do we get rid of toys because children get tired of them; when they reach adolescence, they only have a few soft toys left on the shelf and, at most, a box with their favorites, well kept in the back of the closet.

This time before deciding what to do with them, consider giving them another use. See what more original plant pots can be made by recycling some toy animals. You just need to give it a touch of color, make a hole in the top and place the plant that you like the most. The best succulent, which is tiny and does not require much water.

Bicycle

This idea is classic, surely, we have all seen it before, but it is so beautiful and romantic that I wanted to uncover it. I like it like that; rusty, but also painted from top to bottom; in the garden, leaning against a tree or even hanging on the wall, it doesn't matter; it always looks great! Grab that grungy old bike and dust it off, then fill it with pots. Put one in the front basket part; if you have never had a basket, then great, because its time has come. Change the saddle for a plant that you love and fill the wheels with more and more flowers?

Tires

At Handfie, we love to recycle old tires and make things with them, in this case, a very cool pot for our aloe vera? To create it, join a pair of tires, paint them in color you like best and place a geotextile mesh inside; all you have to do is choose the plant that you like the most.

CHAPTER FIVE
Container Gardening Plan

Container gardening has become the primary go-to method for many people, particularly for people with different physical abilities. Gardening in containers is highly adaptable and can be achieved to make the wider garden experience ready and wait for anyone, even if they're in a wheelchair or have certain physical disabilities that make conventional gardening difficult.

Not only activity in the garden needs to be considered, but convenient access for simple enjoyment also needs to be considered for residents and disabled people who may not enjoy working in a garden but enjoy spending time in the garden. Container gardening makes most physical disabilities a non-issue and opens the hobby to green thumbs and brown thumbs alike.

Container garden preparation requires flexibility, so it works for everyone involved. Simultaneously, the space must be beautiful and well-designed as a coherent landscape. Adhering to traditional garden design and building up usable beds is a good technique, and is simple to do.

When constructing custom raised beds and containers, think about how people can move and operate with plants in them if they are in wheelchairs or walkers. Containers must be mounted in an area providing complete access to the entire container from at least the front and sides. Beds should not be too large and sprawling to fatigue and confuse people. Also, containers and raised beds must be a treat for those who are not physically strong, not a burden. Starting too big can be more like work and drudgery, not an exuberant day out in the garden and enjoying the day.

Using an already formulated soil mix is good practice. Typically, these blends are free of harmful species that can make people sick. They are usually sold in conveniently portable sizes, making adding soil to raised beds simpler. And, it's usually priced dry and not so hard. A fine, high-quality mix also grows plants well.

Fertilizer is preferred. Don't be afraid if you intend to follow the dosing directions on drug bags. Plants grown in containers need plenty of food, particularly plants growing edible harvests like tomatoes and lettuces.

Pest management isn't as simple as soil preparation and fertilization choices. It's not smart to put chemicals into a position where people have poor immune systems and sensitivities that healthy people don't have to think about. Instead, prepare using your hands to patch bugs as you see them or manually delete damaged leaves and stems. Make a gentle insecticide soap to kill indoor bugs like spider mites, aphids, and other common indoor pets. Insecticidal soap can also work well outdoors. Often a sick plant can literally need to be discarded, not trifled.

When picking a container, make sure the gap is not too small because it's hard to plant in. Stop using inferior plastic containers. Glazed ceramic pots are a decent choice, but should have enough holes to drain water. Most wooden containers can rot. Exceptions are cedar and redwood containers.

Use very small containers because they keep plant roots from spreading. When planting deep root vegetables, go into deep containers. Also, think how many plants you want to grow in the jar. Containers should have appropriate drainage holes. Every hole should be at least half an inch in diameter. Cover the pot base with a newspaper so that the soil does not spill from the drainage holes.

If you live in an region with high year-round temperatures, choose light color containers to absorb less heat. Excessive heat absorption leads to root growth. If you want to use clay pots, note that clay doesn't hold moisture well. Check the pots from time to time, so the plants have enough moisture.

Soilless mixtures work best for container gardens. They drain easily, are light in weight, and contain no weeds and pests. Buy these potting mixtures from your nearest nursery. Whenever you put soil in a jar, leave about two inches from the top. This will encourage you to add mulch later.

Many container gardens need about five hours of daylight. For vegetables, root vegetables require more water, while leafy vegetables need less sunlight. Vegetables bearing fruits like tomatoes need full sunshine. Use a low liquid fertilizer while watering your container garden plants. Potting mixtures drain very easily, and if you apply fertilizer as in a normal garden, it continues to drain. Water the plants frequently during the summer months as container plants loose moisture very quickly.

How to Plan Your Container Garden

When you plan a container garden, the first thing to decider is whether you'd rather grow your plants indoors or outdoors. Many people think container gardening is for indoor growing and patios, but containers can be useful for any garden situation.

Containers are perfect for growing almost any plant type, as they offer great flexibility. If you plant your garden in containers and need to move it later, it's quick. Not if you have got a conventional garden!

If you expect really bad weather, you may temporarily move containers to a safer spot, like indoors, garage or basement. But you can't do anything with a conventional garden.

If you see your plants are not doing well because the room you want is too sunny or too dark, you can't do anything with a conventional garden, but you can easily switch potted plants to a better spot.

If you want to have your container garden outside, select a suitable place for it. You'll want to pick a location that has the right amount of sun for the plants you want to grow, but it's also a location that's very open. When working on your garden, it's easy to lose energy if it's several hundred yards from the house!

Place your plants as far from the streets as you can. Car emissions and the dust they kick up will harm and contaminate your plants. You don't want to consume all that waste, so find plants as far from those roads as possible.

If you have your plants indoors, you'll need to pick a really good spot. Most plants must be relatively dry, so if you use air conditioning, you'll need to pick the warmest spot in your building.

Most plants won't do well in very cold homes, so you might need to choose a space for your plants and keep the vent closed in that room to keep it cooler. If you can, choose a bright space with natural sunlight.

Plants flourish with natural light. If you don't have space with plenty of sunshine, use special plant lights for your plants. You can't use any fluorescent lighting as plants won't survive.

You need lights specially designed to grow plants. They provide a broad light spectrum, closer to natural light than regular bulbs. You may also need to change the room humidity with your plants.

Some plants perform best in higher humidity, some in lower humidity. If you raise very fragile or picky plants, you may need to invest in special equipment to change humidity. You probably won't have to do this without developing exotic varieties.

Ultimately, decide whether to organically cultivate your plants. If you're growing indoors, it'll probably be very easy. But if you cultivate your plants outside, the stress of dealing with pests is just too much for you. Don't feel bad if organic gardening is too difficult. You should still try after more practice.

There are thousands of containers for planting. Depending on your budget, certain plants are better than others, and it depends on how you want your garden to look. There are many things to consider when buying containers for your garden.

Once fully grown, the most important thing to consider is how much space your plants will need. Transplanting a near-full-grown plant will shock it seriously enough to die. Ensure the container has sufficient drainage. You don't want your plants to sink by mistake or rain from overwatering. If you cultivate edible plants, make sure the material isn't poisonous to people (or animals). This can be a wood-treated problem.

You may want to consider positioning them on a wheeled platform or dolly for large containers, and for easier travel. So you can push your big plants quickly and easily to take advantage of the sun or keep them out of the heat.

Most household products can be recycled to plant containers to save money and benefit the ecosystem. This can make a special, sexy look, depending on what you're using. Include cut-off milk jugs, detergent jugs, styrofoam containers and coolers, cinder blocks, drainage pipe and everything else around the building. Decorate your home-made containers with paints, permanent markers, ribbons or whatever you want. Know that containers have a lot to do with your container garden's attractiveness.

CHAPTER SIX
Fruit and Vegetables in Pots

Growing your own vegetables and aromatic herbs is tempting, especially when the weather is good. Who doesn't want to go for a walk in their garden and pick the day's juicy vegetables to make their meal? Unfortunately, if you don't have a small garden well known as a vegetable garden or worse if you don't have a garden at all, then the vision ends there.

It is here the planters come in. A large number of valued, edible plants are growing in pots. So wherever you want you can put them: in a garden, on a terrace or even on a balcony.

Please note that there are a few basic rules to follow. Next, your planter needs to be the right size to fit the plant you have selected. Lettuces, spinach, and aromatic herbs need little space. By contras, the tomatoes and peppers are round, yes.

Many basic rules: the use of "special edible plants in containers" for potting soil encourages plant growth in the planter. The garden soil should be avoided because it is too thick. You should also know that watering frequency is more critical in pot-growing than in a patch of vegetables. Indeed, as is the case in open land, the roots won't have the possibility to leave the pot to receive water.

Finally, if you put the plants on a balcony, make sure it supports the weight, and no condominium regulations forbid the planting! Small containers are typically not a problem, but it would be a shame if your laurel planter fell onto the patio below your neighbor.

If you want 100% organic fruits and vegetables, you can choose to have your own greenhouse. You can control what goes into an increasing phase. You can, for example, avoid using chemically rich composts and fertilizers and use organic ones.

A big factor in growing your own fruits and vegetables is the place you want to plant them. Choosing a spot where there's plenty of sunshine is always important. While different temperature zones exist, each zone has its own unique range to expand. Yes, as long as you do things right while you work, you will be able to produce your own organic goods.

Typically, growing vegetables in a pot are done on the balcony. However, in order to realize this idea, you need to comply with the requirements of the plants and the exposure of the balcony. If it is shaded for most of the day, you cannot grow a light-loving plant, even if the exposure is south. So take a close look at the requirements of the vegetables we present to you and decide what to grow on your terrace.

Space is not a limitation for growing fruits and vegetables

You can have a big garden or a small plot. Even you could live in a garden-free flat or home. There are several different gardening techniques and methods that allow you to do it almost anywhere.

For example, container gardening allows you to grow fruits and vegetables in a small greenhouse, patio, and balcony. These containers can easily grow dwarf fruit trees. Tomatoes, cucumbers, onions, and herbs can be cultivated in small containers.

Here are some advantages of container gardening:

- Besides helping you to grow your own organic vegies and fruits, they can also be a good decorative device. Imagine getting a dwarf apple tree on your tiny patio full of apples. How cool and stunning to the eyes.

- They can be easily handled and maintained. With your garden in a large pot, you don't have to worry about high maintenance jobs to keep your garden clean.

- They're very mobile, a big benefit. You can quickly change your container garden's location if it doesn't get enough sunlight. If you ever move to another town, you can take it with you.

So, whether you stay in a large garden house or in a flat with no garden at all, different gardening approaches will match your circumstances. You can cultivate your own organic fruit and vegetables.

Ten easy-to-grow fruit and vegetable varieties in pots

- **Aromatic herbs**

Herbs are pleasant in pots of all sizes, placed on a window sill or along an aisle. For herbs of the mint family, it is strongly advised to plant them in a planter if you do not want your garden to be completely invaded in the years to come.

The trick to planting potted herbs is to choose containers that can accommodate the adult plant. Smaller herbs such as chervil, chives, cilantro, marjoram, oregano, parsley, sage, savory, tarragon and thyme can be grown in planters 15 to 30 cm deep and 30 cm maximum width. Basil, lavender and lemongrass will work best in pots of 40 to 45 cm minimum and rosemary and dill in larger planters. As for the bay leaf, start with a 45 cm pot before replanting it in the garden, or prune it to control its growth.

- **Salads**

Salads are also easy to grow in pots since most varieties have shallow roots. Placing them in a raised container like an old wheelbarrow allows them to be highlighted rather than ignored, as is often the case with plants that grow on the ground. You can only plant one type of salad per pot or mix it up. You will need a pot 15 cm deep for most lettuces, mixed greens and green vegetables, as well as 20 cm for endives, chicory and spinach.

- **Strawberries**

What a pleasure to see your strawberries growing and watching the stems grow heavy under the weight of the fruit! By placing them in pots, you can put them wherever you want and pick some for a gourmet break in your garden or on your terrace. And why not grow your strawberries in a hanging pot? This will have the advantage of keeping snails and slugs away. A strawberry planter is a must, and strawberries are not difficult to grow. It is enough to place them in a depth of soil of at least 20 centimeters. If you plant them in a hanging basket, opt for a larger pot with a width and a depth of about 30 centimeters.

The strawberry delight especially well in pots and in the sun. The advantage is that once planted, and they give beautiful fruits every year without taking care of them. You can vary the early and late varieties to have them throughout the summer.

Figure 5 - Strawberries

These plants are easy to plant. They don't require space nor a lot of maintenance and adapt perfectly to the culture in the pot on a balcony. Strawberries and raspberries are ideal for growing on the edge of a window. Plant of strawberries or raspberries in a pot about 30-40 cm in diameter and depth. Fill the pan with potting soil on a background lined with gravel and place the tray of strawberries or raspberries in full sun. Water frequently to keep the soil slightly moist.

- **Peppers**

Although pepper is a vegetable that grows very well in a vegetable patch, sowing in a pot will allow you to start growing earlier. You sow them in pots placed in a protected place, and then you can replant them in your vegetable patch, where they will take advantage of the heat of summer to ripen. The only problem with peppers grown in planters is that they rarely reach the size of vegetables planted in a vegetable patch. But they remain just as tasty and will bring wonderful touches of color to your balcony or patio. Your planter should be at least 20 cm deep (30 cm deep is optimal) and be 40 to 45 cm wide.

Peppers have a great pot yield and have no problem growing in a small space. They just need sun and warmth. A pot at least 30 cm deep, soil drained with a little fertilizer at the time of planting, and voila.

- **Tomatoes**

Tomatoes planted in pots are just as tasty as tomatoes in the ground. This type of culture also has an advantage if you live in an area where there are soil-borne plant diseases. Plant your tomatoes in pots and renew the soil every year, so you won't have to worry about the rotation of your crops. Once you have found the ideal location for your tomatoes, you can place them in the same place from one year to the next.

As with other edible plants, you will need to make sure your planter matches the size of your adult tomato plants. My advice is to think big, because even small cherry tomatoes will need a pot or hanging basket at least 30 centimeters deep and wide, while varieties of large tomatoes will need to be planted in a pot. Although the sight of the branches of tomatoes overflowing from your planter is a real pleasure for the eyes, it is recommended to provide stakes for varieties of large tomatoes.

For their normal development require 18-30 degrees. If the temperature is below 15 degrees, flowering stops. Due to the heat above 30 degrees, the leaves remain small, and the branches of the stems thin. It is possible to drop the colors. At below 15 and above 40 degrees, no dye is formed, and the fruits turn yellowish. High temperatures cause sunburn on the fruit if the leaves do not shade them. If the terrace is shady, your tomatoes will not rise, they love the sun. Vegetables need moisture - the soil moisture should be above 70-80% and 50-60% air. Tomatoes are demanding on the soil. Their root system develops deep, so prepare a large pot (maybe a tin of cheese, but it won't be pretty). Fill it with nutrient-rich soil mix: two parts of well-burned manure and one part of the soil. Consider your balcony options and plant tomatoes. Regularly water and nourish with sherbet.

- **Eggplants**

Eggplants are often overlooked in vegetable gardens and planters adorning modern balconies. It's a shame because the plant is beautiful and offers beautiful purple flowers in spring, then sparkling fruits of purple (which come in variations of white, green, red and yellow). Eggplants are not very large but need room to grow well. Choose a planter about 30 cm deep and

40 to 45 cm wide, then give it a place of honor among your other pots.

- **Potatoes**

If you make a list of plants suitable for planting in pots, potatoes will certainly be absent. However, a potato planter is quite feasible as long as you opt for a large container, such as a barrel cut in half, for example. The procedure: rather than burying your potatoes to the desired depth, plant shallowly, then add potting soil as the tubers grow. Planting them in a barrel makes this easier. And while the tubers are growing, you can still admire and benefit from the green plant with its pale-colored flowers.

- **Zucchini**

Summer squash, especially compact varieties like this patisson, can be controlled in terms of their size when grown in pots. Thus, you will no longer have to search under kilometers of oversized leaves to find your zucchini, not easily visible unless they reach the size of Godzilla. Another piece of advice: prefer non-staked varieties rather than climbing plants, unless you want to set up a trellis. Either way, you won't be able to get by with tiny pots facing these high-growing plants. Instead, opt for a pot of 45 cm in diameter for each zucchini plant, or even larger.

It is very easy to grow, and they benefit from having rapid growth and very pretty flowers. You can plant zucchini in a tray PVC or metal of at least 60 cm diameter. Fill it with soil rich in organic matter. Place in full sun sheltered from the wind and water regularly.

The zucchini delight pot are easier to maintain than squash. It is one of the easiest vegetables to grow in pots on a balcony or patio. They will give you generous and abundant fruit if they are in full sun. Choose a variety of "non-runner" and small fruits like the "round of Nice."

- **Dwarf beans**

Technically, the most common variety of snap beans can grow in a planter, but dwarf beans are better choices because they are smaller. There are many varieties. Look for rather large containers, but be aware that if you only have a depth of 15 centimeters, this will not prevent the success of your harvest. If you opt for climbing beans, add stakes when planting. Beans can be grown in pots but require a pan large and deep (40 cm minimum) because it produces many fine roots. Plant your beans in a compost garden that is light and well-drained so that the roots do not rot. Green beans blossomed quickly alongside strawberries, carrots, cabbage, and cucumbers. Do not hesitate to involve them in one large bin.

- **Lemons**

Figure 6- Lemon tree

You may live in a region where the winters are cold, but rest assured, this will not prevent you from growing your own lemons or limes, oranges or kumquats. You will just have to make sure to plant them in a pot exposed to outside light in summer, and placed in a shelter or in your house in winter. You can start with a fairly small pot when your tree is young, but be aware that you will then have to replant it in a larger pot at least 45 centimeters deep and wide. To be able to move the pot, place it on a roller base. You will be able to make your own citrus juice, even if you live in Dunkirk.

- **Cucumbers - on the northeast terrace**

The cucumber is very heat-loving and water-loving. Plants grow well at 25-30 degrees Celsius and high humidity of 90%. At below 15 degrees, growth stops. It is slightly demanding of light and develops relatively well when shaded.

The root system is weak and superficial, so you should water it regularly. Drought during flowering and flopping adds color and knotting, and the cucumbers are deformed. Low soil and air humidity make them bitter. Vegetables are extremely demanding on soil and air humidity. Prepare the fertilizer-soil mixture, fill it in chests and sow the seeds in a radish 10-15 cm distance and 3-4 cm deep. Regularly water and nourish with sherbet. A warm northeast balcony with more watering and nourishment will reward you with fresh vegetables for your favorite tarator.

- **Lettuce**

The lettuce grows very quickly, thereby is often harvested throughout the season. In general, it is sown in the spring, but beware, it fears frost. So, depending on your region, wait for the right time to sow it. To grow it, you need a large but shallow pot. Leave a space of about 10 cm between each future salad. Depending on the lettuce varieties, they take up more or less space. For example, the "Appia" lettuce produces a large head while the "Sloth" spreads with large green leaves. Always keep the soil moist and well-drained.

- **Radishes**

The radishes are really suitable for pot culture. In addition, in 3 weeks, the harvest is already there. You can grow them in pots of any size. 15 cm deep is enough, or more if you can, but remember to leave them a little space between them.

- **Shanghai Cabbage**

Shanghai cabbage is perfectly suited for growing in pots because it is not bulky. In addition, it does not need a lot of suns: the morning sun is enough (about 3 hours a day). Consider putting natural fertilizer on them regularly and keeping the soil moist.

- **Kale**

The kale is perfectly suited to container culture. Harvest the young leaves at once, or let it grow and harvest it several times. Kale likes cool places, and it becomes bitter in hot weather. Depending on your region, plant it in the sun (for cool regions) and in a semi-shaded area (warm region).

- **Mustard greens**

The mustard greens like heat and have an advantage: they require no care. Put them in a medium pot, in full sun. Choose the variety of mustard you prefer: the "Dragon Tongue" is purplish and rather sweet, while the "Green wave" is strong and spicy. Choose the large leaves for cooking in curry, and the young shoots for salads.

- **Garlic**

The garlic bulbs are quite expensive, but they have so many health benefits that we should not do without. And then, growing them yourself in pots is very economical. You can cook the bulbs, but also the leaves in salads. Choose a pot at least 20 cm deep and wide enough to leave 15 cm between each bulb.

CHAPTER SEVEN
Vertical Planting System

The vertical vegetable garden is the answer to growing vegetables in a small space. The idea was born especially for those who live in the city and do not have a plot of land but only a small garden, if not simply a little space on the terrace or balcony. Those in these conditions are normally forced to give up the pleasure of growing their favorite vegetables, putting aside their green thumb and the idea of bringing something self-produced to the table.

Fortunately, these people come across the vertical vegetable garden, which, as the name suggests, takes advantage of the vertical space by arranging the containers with the sowing in height on different shelves. Obviously, there are some rules to follow, and you can't just stack the pots at random.

Another excellent idea, if you have space, includes running a partition right to the fence. This gives more plant-growing surfaces. Cover certain surfaces with wire or trellises, using planting boxes for root crops on other surfaces.

You won't need a large plot for trellis vegetable gardening. Even if you just have a walkway and fence, in planters, you can cultivate some plants, or anywhere you can build a trellis. If you have room, use the ground for root crops such as beets and carrots, and as I said, grow wine on trellises or fences or walls.

Don't push the first year too hard. Put in a few crops and enjoy trellis planting, rather than attempting to grow so many vegetables that planting becomes a chore. You can grow vegetables parallel to fences or walls directly in the ground wherever you can install a trellis-or use planter.

How you do depends on the area's room and character. If I have a patio, gardening in containers is far easier. When you grow other plants in a small garden area, growing in the ground with trellis support will harmonize better with the overall scheme.

You can also expand flower gardens vertically. You can grow fruit trees with great success vertically. Most berries are climbers and thus suitable for vertical gardening.

Types of vertical gardening

There are different options for growing a vertical garden. Here's what they are:

1. Growth in a vertical container

You can buy or buy vertical container gardens. If you want to create your own, you need to create a frame with slats.

From there, you will see large windows that will easily attach to the frame. You can plant and grow vertically very easily.

Although you can also use a similar configuration for the sake of simplicity.

In both cases, the containers offer you the possibility of growing a variety of vegetables in a compact manner.

2. Pocket Gardening

You can create your own canvas pocket garden with a fabric canvas. You sew pockets into the canvas pocket, or you can use it for the sake of simplicity.

However, you can also buy one.

Either way, landscaped gardens allow those who have no room for growth to be able to grow something, provided they have a sunny wall.

3. wall planters

Wall planters are basic planters that attach to a wall and make it easier to grow different varieties of flowers or vegetables.

Again, it's easy to grow vegetables when you don't have a growing space, but rather a balcony wall or a divider between living spaces in urban areas.

4. Pallet planter

is an inexpensive way to grow a vertical garden. There are several ways to convert a pallet to a planter.

However, I used a palette to grow a herb garden. I used old jugs of milk and hung them on the pallet with the handle of the pitcher. It was inexpensive and simple to create.

5. shelves

is a great option for a vertical garden because it expands your horizons. You can plant a container garden and put all the containers on the shelf.

It will be easier to plant more varieties of vegetables in a compact space.

6. Hanging basket

are another great way to broaden your horizons with vertical gardening. You can grow tomatoes and other fruit plants that would otherwise be hard to grow in a pocket on a wall.

7. trellis

Finally, you can wall. A trellis wall will facilitate the cultivation of vegetables with long vines such as cucumbers or green beans. The trellis will allow the plants to grow instead of going out. This facilitates their growth in a compact space.

How to grow a vertical garden

Growing a vertical garden is more complicated than other varieties of gardening. The reason is that plants should be encouraged to grow differently from what they usually are. That said, here is what you need to know to grow your own vertical garden:

1. Where will he go?

The advantage of a vertical garden is that it can go anywhere. You can grow it outside on a balcony or a separation wall.

You can also grow a vertical garden indoors.

But you can also grow a vertical garden that goes outside when it's hot and indoors when it's cold. You will need to find a way to wheel your vertical garden or make it easy to move from base to base.

Again, if you want a vertical hybrid garden, using shelving is the easiest and probably the cheapest method.

2. Choose your plants

There are a few important options that you need to consider when deciding what to plant in your vertical garden.

First, you will need to choose flexible plants. If you choose plants, such as dwarf fruit trees or blueberries to place in a vertical garden, they branch out.

This will make your vertical garden spread out over the verses. This defies the whole purpose of your garden being compact.

In short, you need to choose plants that will flow easily (especially if you are creating a garden with vertical pockets).

Naturally, your options open up if you decide to use shelves with containers or hanging baskets.

Then you need to choose plants that have similar needs. You usually don't have the ease of moving vertical gardens.

With this in mind, you need to plant vegetation that can withstand full sun or needs a lot of shade.

3. Good soil is a must

As you plant vegetables in an area other than the soil, they will not have the opportunity to draw nutrients from a large amount of soil around them.

In fact, they will have very little land around them. This is why it is essential to use quality potting soil when planting your vegetables.

4. Start your plants

Then you have to go somewhere other than the vertical garden. A vertical garden has a gravity that always pulls on it. This makes it difficult to develop healthy roots.

For this reason, you should start your plants indoors until they are in full bloom. When the plants are vigorous, you can plant them in the vertical garden.

At this point, they should be able to manage gravity by pulling on them as they grow.

5. water frequently

You should be sure of yourself. Plants have shallow roots due to limited growing space.

Also, they don't have much soil to help them retain moisture. These two factors make it difficult for a plant to retain water indefinitely.

Water is a great way to water a vertical garden that sits on a wall, such as a folding garden.

6. Need for fertilizer

Plants growing in a vertical garden cannot get nutrients from the soil around them because they are not planted in the soil.

With that in mind, realize that your plants will have to be. This will give them the nutrients they need to thrive. You can feed them by hand with a liquid fertilizer in a sprayer or include them in the irrigation system when watering.

7. Plant insurance

Finally, you will need to keep adding plants on hand, as some plants will die in a vertical garden. This happens because plants have a shallow root system.

However, when the plants in your vertical garden begin to die, their appeal is less attractive. It is a good idea to grow additional plants and keep them in other containers.

This way, when a plant dies, you can extract the dead and put a healthy one back in the vertical paradise of your vegetable patch.

Benefits of the vertical garden

Before finishing, we would like to talk to you about some of the advantages of installing a vertical garden in your house. Take note!

- It starts you on self-consumption: this way you will know where the food you eat comes from and you will start to have a much more natural diet.
- It unites you as a family: because you can organize new activities, both planting and creating more space.
- It is a very healthy activity: it not only stimulates your imagination, but also allows you to exercise outdoors and stay active.

Vertical Gardening With Vegetables

A vertical garden is a method of cultivation above ground, which allows growing vegetables, and plants in general, stage by stage. The principle is to be able to cultivate everywhere, without necessarily having space on the ground, as long as you benefit from correct sunshine and a little water.

Unlike a horizontal vegetable patch, the vertical vegetable patch allows you to produce as much or even more over a smaller area. The culture can be done in soil or in an inert substrate (sand, clay balls). It is possible to have a vertical vegetable garden for a few euros for a simple system, and a few hundred euros for larger and automated systems.

The vertical vegetable garden is often done outside, but can very well be set up inside in an apartment, as long as you have a bright window. The small footprint and the ease of cultivation make it a real trend for years to come. Produce at home, anywhere, without space, just with the desire to eat vegetables and aromatics "from the garden".

VERTICAL GARDENING is tested to grow vegetables. If you have a clear understanding of vertical gardening concepts and the few criteria vegetables really need to grow, you're more likely to have a good experience with your vertical garden.

Root Space Is Key

Usually, vertical gardens have more limited root space than those on the ground, so find a system that has plenty of root room for your vegetables and you'll be off to a great start. If you've ever grown vegetables in containers, you'll know how critical it is to keep soil temperatures and moisture levels as even as possible. Plants that are stressed of heat or water quickly lose vigor; in these conditions, vegetables often 'rocket' to seed, resulting in very low growth.

Triple Your Existing Growing Space

Yeah, yeah ... The use of a soil-based, vertical garden system is a perfect option for space-restricted gardeners. Growing a large pot garden takes up plenty of floor space. Vertical garden systems actually build planting space; you can triple your area's square meter by going vertically and harvesting abundantly!

No Pots - No Trays!

Compared to pots and many other vertical gardening systems, soil volumes in steel vertical systems are massive. In this vertical gardening method, plant roots can move over half a cubic meter of soil media thickness. This large volume of soil helps greatly maintain even temperatures and humidity levels, thussaving time and energy compared to other vertical gardening systems and other planters.

Looking Good

Your vegetables excel in this vertical garden system, but they also look stunning. Your vertical garden will become a feature in any space; a living green wall that embellishes and feeds the whole family! In restricted areas, aesthetics are so critical, but everybody deserves fresh salad!

Feeding Tips

Thanks to the wide body of soil media in the open tiered, steel vertical gardening method, plants may benefit from a wide nutrient supply. Regular feeding with conventional watering liquid fertilizers and some slow release fertilizer a few times a year, is all that is required.

No Moving Parts

Many vertical gardening systems are focused on hydroponic growing methods where plants are anchored to matting or foam and have additional systems to monitor irrigation and fertilizer solution applications; however, the open tiered, steel vertical gardening system is based on a conventional low-tech gardening experience. This vertical garden is lined with soil media (potting mix) from top to bottom, and basically you only plant your favorite vegetable seeds or seedlings with your trowel into the exposed potting media and water them in. Water your vertical garden with collected rain or mains water with any tool you want, such as watering pipe, hose or automatic dripper system.

Like vegetables, herbs also like moisture and temperature levels, so building a broad root mass is essential to your success, and vertical gardening is the perfect solution. Herbs love growing in vertical gardens with a quality potting mix rather than felt or foam types of green walls; so herbs react very well in an open, steel vertical gardening system. Moreover, due to the increased root space available compared to conventional planting methods, many gardeners find that in the open tiered, steel vertical gardening system, herbs perform better than they ever have in pots!The varieties of herbs you select in a vertical garden will depend on your tastes and appearance. For Asian herbs, select coriander, lemongrass and mint. Maybe your kitchen is more Italian, and you want to grow garlic, basil and oregano. It should be remembered that some herbs are perennial, and last year for a year, others are annuals or biennials, and will have to be replaced annually by seeds or cuttings. Regardless of the transplanting method you choose, an open-layer vertical steel gardening system is suitable as you simply grow your garden in a potting mix-as usual. Perhaps using smaller plants or seeds is cheaper, so you'll save time by having fun growing your own plants from scratch.

If you have little water available in your vertical garden, plant the tougher Mediterranean style herbs like curry plant, rosemary, sage, oregano and thymes. Whether your vertical garden has more security and/or water storage, you can also plant the slightly more delicate herbs like coriander, basil, parsley.

Some herbs are so vigorous, they will overwhelm the tenderer varieties in your vertical garden. Be warned that planting in the mint family or lemon balm is likely to spread and drown the other herbs in your vertical garden.

Whether in a vertical garden or not, herbs love daily picking to encourage fresh, flavorful, tip production. The more you choose, the more you get; so even if you don't want to eat herbs, prune frequently to keep plants healthy and ample supply.

Use rainwater or water to keep your soil-based, open tiered, vertical garden in good shape. Either hand water as needed, or use a simple automated dripper device to take care of watering when away or forgetting.

Vertical herb gardening is deliciously simple, a wonderful activity to share with grandchildren and give you an attractive, aromatic, year-round abundance of culinary joy! After you've tasted the difference, dried stuff will never return to the musty 'past use by date.'

CHAPTER EIGHT
Raised Bed Gardening

If you enjoy eating fresh organic vegetables but don't like pulling weeds or running up a big water bill with a conventional row garden, then you'll enjoy square foot gardening. Square foot gardening is performed in a 4-foot garden bed consisting of four side panels and no edge. You'll need a weed barrier to build the edge. Instead you fill the bed with a special soil mix: three equal parts of vermiculite (to retain moisture), peat moss (to make the soil light and drain loose), and compost (for nutrients). You can find these in your nearest nursery or garden shop. If you're eager to get started right away, just buy the commercial compost now. But it will do well to start making your own organic compost later. It's a smart way to use your kitchen vegetable scraps and lawn clippings as well as save money on industrial fertilizer.

Raised bed gardening, square foot gardening is often named. The original idea was to increase the gardens' growth and yield. This form of plantation often decreases the use of water and is a perfect way to grow a garden in low soil areas.

You start by building a simple four-foot-square raised bed. A bed of this size makes it easy from either side to reach the middle. Use timber eight to 12 inches generally, so your bed is lifted tall. Put the fresh ground in the house. You're going to want to add some fertilizer slow down. It feeds your plants in the summer and helps increase your crop growth.

You can plant your raised bed in many ways. You can divide the bed by string in a foot by a foot. This gives you nine equal spaces for development. This portion is suitable for small crops such as onions, herbs and so on. You will only want one or two plants per segment if you grow plants that have bigger plants, such as tomatoes.

Another alternative is to split the bed evenly into two. It's a perfect way to grow corn, beans and potatoes. Wide spreading crops such as tomatoes, pumpkins, and watermelons will each need their own bed so they have room to spread.

When planting your fields, consider how big every plant eventually gets. You don't want smaller plants like corn shading. Keep your plants grouped big to tiny, and plant north to south.

This method of planting allows plants to grow closer together, growing the space that weeds need to grow. Near planting also tends to shade the soil, retaining moisture longer and helping to conserve water. The plants are well fertilized from the slow-release fertilizer you first mixed in the soil, and they have enough water. They also get plenty of light by paying attention to their size when planting.]

Reasons To Consider Building A Raised Bed Garden

Perfect Soil

There is a raised garden above your current level of soil where you fill the soil you want. Then, you can get the exact perfect soil your plants need to grow and make sure it's perfectly balanced, so your plants get the best chance for lush growth.

Better Drainage

Since the soil you place in your raised bed is looser than the natural soil in your backyard, the raised garden has much more drainage than the majority of gardens. Drainage is necessary to successfully grow plants since most plants can not grow in standing water.

Higher Yield

If you want to grow more plants in the same room, it's a great way to create a raised bed garden. You can plant the plants in a raised garden closer together because the beds are designed so that you don't have to enter between the plants for maintenance. Closer growth of the plants means more plants per square foot.

Easy Maintenance

Raised bed gardens are easier to maintain as every floor in the bed can easily be reached. The idea was to build your bed so that it doesn't have a limit of 4 feet long at any point and then point it at least 2 feet away if you have more than one bed. So you can easily touch any plant from outside the bed and you have an aisle to go in, without having to go into the bed to plumb, harvest or care for your plants otherwise. It also makes weeding and putting down mulch much easier.

Less Soil Compaction

Since the raised bed is easier to maintain and doesn't allow you to walk through the rows of plants for maintenance, soil compaction should be much less meaning, so that the plants have more growth opportunities and fewer break-up opportunities.

Creating a raised bed garden isn't that difficult. What you need is some kind of material to make the 4 sides, and you can use boards or specially-made beds that you can buy in the garden shop. A raised garden can be any height, but make sure yours is at least 6 inches off the ground.

Some people now use very large waistbands that allow them to grow plants very easily, and if you are able to plant them all standing, it is much easier on their knees. Such elevated gardens are ideal for both vegetables and flowers, and are a perfect way to add height and scale to your landscape.

Advantages of Raised Beds Gardening

Gardening on raised beds provides some important advantages over conventional agriculture, which allows it to be used to grow ornamental plants and naturally, vegetables for many years. Raised beds help to resolve unadapted soils and terrain, and provide a way for people with back and knee issues to start gardening.

When designing our plant garden we look for three important requirements in the garden: plenty of sunshine, good soil and good drainage; and of course, a rich supply of water. Although we can place our garden to full sunlight every day, the consistency of the soil can not always be managed, and unsuitable land can be costly and not necessarily practical. Here, lifted beds can solve most of our difficulties.

If the soil is founded on clay and very firm and has low drainage in the only place you need, a raised bed alleviates the problem that the water is slowly draining through the bed. A slight excavation full of gravel or coarse rocks can help with drainage problems if your only option is the boggy water field. Building high-rise beds on steep slopes is a good way to use wasted space and beds often avoid sloping erosion using the runoff in your beds.

Raised beds allow you to maximize room for cultivation because rows are removed, and you can still reach the plants on the back when making beds up to four feet deep. This gardening method allows a greater number of plants to be grown than a traditional garden allows, and helps to control weeds due to the shade of good plants.

Raised garden beds can be made from old lumber or railway sleepers found or bought; should be at least about 12 inches tall and can be made up to waist height if materials allow or if you have back or knee problems. For the selfish gardener with a weak back, raised beds will keep them doing what they enjoy. If the stakes are driven into the ground to support them, old fence palings or floor boards can also be used.

Very little ground preparation is needed before the bed is built; the grass is managed by a few layers of ancient press and if the ground is 12-inch deeper or larger, the field may shock the grass before reaching the surface. A high stake in every corner stops the plants from damaging when the pants are pulled over your pillow.

The raised beds should warm up much more quickly in the spring and dry up quickly after heavy rain; this ensures optimal plant growth conditions. The only downside with raised beds is that in extremely hot weather, they can dry up faster and need to be watered often. For portable shade cloth coverings, this can be minimized even on particularly hot days.

Planting is still a popular hobby for both families and couples, but smaller lots or no lots have sparked interest in raised bed planting. This famous gardening method enables the cultivation of fresh fruit and vegetables in small areas, just a few meters away. As knowledge of eating grows locally, locals spread the word; a small amount of fresh food grows in a small plot.

Soil dispersed over ground heats up more rapidly in the spring, which allows for better seeding opportunities. Most gardeners face challenging conditions in the soil. Heavy clay or light sandy soils are rising under conditions that even the most experienced gardener is frustrated. Raised bed planting allows the grower to blend the recet for optimal growth with the best ingredients. Top land, compost, mouths and nutrients allow healthy plants to grow on denser plantings that reduce the inflammation of weeds.

Garden size depends on how much raised bed planting you want to do. Keeping the bed four feet wide allows easy access from both sides. A six-to-eight-inch bed depth is suggested because most of the major feeder roots are at this depth. Locate the bed in full sun if possible; if not, at least half a day of sunlight is required for good plant growth. A water supply should be nearby, as raised bed gardens dry out faster than traditional gardening.

CONCLUSION

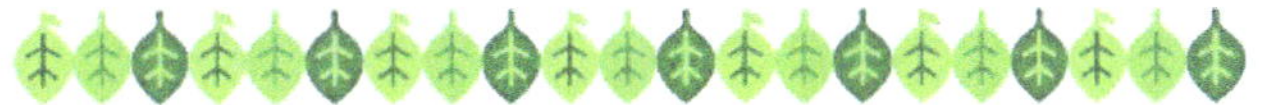

If you're among that number of people who want to turn to container gardening, then you're right. There's plenty of useful information on this new form of gardening here.

Millions worldwide are seeking container gardening these days. With its many advantages, nothing comes as a surprise. Indeed, many wonder why they haven't tried it years ago.

One of the key advantages of this style of gardening is that you don't need a sprawling garden to try. Since all plants will be planted in containers, you can build it according to any room available in your home. Additionally, you can also arrange and then rearrange the containers to fit them with your house's interiors.

Container gardening is popular for another cause, accessibility. For starters, plants are easier for the elderly. They can touch and tend plants quickly. Via this special yet realistic idea, disabled people can also enjoy their share of gardening.

Soil quality is another reason many seek container gardening. Since you can grow plants in containers, you can always ensure good soil quality. It's not always that you grow plants in a traditional garden. Additionally, you also have the option to change the soil with the containers if at any time you feel the quality is not good and substitute it at your convenience.

With plants growing in a container feeding them, it is much simpler. You can easily use fertilizers and live with plants. It also means that the fertilizer or pesticide you use is not wasted and benefits the plants.

If you grow plants in a greenhouse, you always experience an extended growing season. You're no longer at the mercy of the environment, and you can seek to cultivate different plants easily from the comforts of your home. With so many benefits, container gardening is finding an increasing number of takers these days.

RAISED BED GARDENING

An Easy Guide to Growing Organic Vegetables
with Your Thriving Raised Bed Garden
Month by Month

INTRODUCTION

Growing plants in raised beds have many advantages. One of the greatest benefits is the ability to produce more from the same area. In addition, elevated bed gardens can improve the amount of space harvested for produce. As a result, the area footage required for the crop is considerably reduced, and more space can be dedicated to plants.

An advantage of growing in elevated beds is changing the soil quality more readily and growing plants in barren soil. However, growing in it can be difficult if your garden is typically very sandy or you have lots of clay. But if you have a raised bed, you can simply put your own purchased or created soil mix in the frame and grow your plants.

Weeds are often much less a concern in the traditional elevated bed. Since the soil is limited, any weeds that pop up are easier to find, and the weed seeds in the current soil are buried under just too much soil to sprout in most cases.

Gardening is no longer limited to greenhouses or yard-houses. Today, you can quickly build an indoor beautiful and serene garden. Many people now use them for indoor gardening. These beds are suitable for fruit plants, flowers, and vegetables. Also, the height of the beds decreases the back pressure you get when dealing with traditional gardens with constant bending.

The design of higher garden beds is an excellent way for new gardeners to green their fingers. Easier to manage than traditional beds lifted beds can take you from the safety of the garden or garden path – without worrying about pushing your flowerbed soil underfoot. This is able to compress the soil around the roots of your plants, raising their air contact to grow.

A combination of soil and compost can be used on a raised garden bed, eliminating from the garden the risk of 'poor dirt,' an issue that faces multiple gardeners in urban areas. With raised bed gardening, Water Drainage is more effective, making the plants easier to respire once again.

Raised Garden Beds are garden beds that are raised above the surrounding soil or ground on which they are constructed and are typically supported by some kind of frame. These frames can be made of different materials, blocks, bricks, stones, or wood. A hung garden bed can also be seen as an uplifting bed.

With the comfort that the garden does not normally exceed 4 feet in, and for any duration, the height of the raised bed is set. The 4-foot-dimension is because one can touch from both sides the middle of the garden. A downside with a bed that's long is that when performing a specific task that involves the entire bed width, such as planting or weeding, it makes for a long walk around the Gardens Bed. 4 feet by 8 feet high garden bed is usually considered to be a suitable size for most gardeners, both for gardening and for 8 feet, which is a standard wooden size that can be purchased at most lumberyards.

One major advantage is that the amount of edge available is increased by dividing a long garden bed into a shorter portion. There is a definition of permaculture that needs to be identified or to understand the "edge effect" and the interaction between two media, the intersection of which meet different environments. This interaction between two different ecosystems provides a broader range of favorable environmental conditions that improve both the life of the animals and plants.

Raised beds also have the ability to plant crops closer together because they don't have to spacewalking paths, and so the traditional walking method is more productive per square foot.

The benefits of higher-density planting are also that plants grow together, shade exposed soil, and suppress weed growth.

A raised bed garden would also benefit from the opportunity to maintain a better soil condition. Due to the easy access of an elevated gardens' bed, no compaction is found in the soil that is normally caused by walking in the conventional row gardening method. If the soil is changed with organic matter, the natural life of the soil will function.

CHAPTER ONE

Vegetal Garden Planning

Starting a new project is always a good idea, with a simple plan in mind. Map out a plan for the vegetable garden based on the desired result you like. Consider your family size, and then work on the premise that it takes about 100 square meters to feed a family of four during the year. First, consider the climatic conditions in which you live; you can not grow vegetables all year round if it is cold. The garden that you design will need to be bigger in this case so you can grow extra vegetables.

The climate is generally divided into dry, temperate and tropical when planning a vegetable garden. You will need to do some research on the type of climate conditions prevailing in your part of the world and the vegetables that thrive in this environment. That is the perfect way to design a vegetable garden. You will move on to the next part of the plan once you have a plan and know what vegetables to produce and how to layout the garden.

Identify and order a good store for your seeds long before planting time, so you're ready to grow when it starts. With organic gardening techniques, you can opt to germinate the seeds separately and then plant them as seedlings. When you have large plantings on your list, schedule the germination of the seeds, so you don't end up maturing all of them at the same time.

Now you have to concentrate on the program, growing vegetables to grow in your garden. Each plant has different needs, and you will have to consider that when planning your vegetable garden. In colder climates, plants that can survive frost include cauliflower, turnips, brussels sprouts, broccoli, snow peas and onions.

A mild disposition is essential for vegetables, including carrots, parsnips, leek, salads, celery and cod. If you try to develop them out of season, you might end up with nothing for your table. The warm seasonal vegetables like potatoes, tomatoes, eggplants, beans, corn and capsicums do not live and die. Most of their growth will be in warm weather months.

You will do your own research and decide exactly what to develop and when. Don't let nurseries talk about buying seeds that won't yield anything because planting them is the wrong time of year. Find the following gardening tips while preparing your garden.

- The cool winds stun your plant growth, and the hot winds dry out the soil and damage the plants, and the plants are destroyed by extra-strong winds. To protect the plants, you may have to prepare a windbreak.

- It takes at least five hours of sunshine every day when you find your yard, so you have direct sunlight.

- Taller plants should not be positioned where smaller plants obstruct the sunlight. Before you start planting, monitoring the sun's path through your garden may not be a bad idea.

- Structure up your compost stack and proceed to top it, it is the easiest way to naturally fertilize your garden. Plant rotation is nice as it does not give the pests much chance to invade the crop.

How to Plan a Vegetable Garden

Many of us, just a sketch, would have drawn our gardens to decide the room we have and help us choose the plants we would grow. To ensure the time you spend preparing your garden is as successful as possible, there are a few main questions to ask yourself.

A well-designed garden with a raised bed

Many of us will have drawn our gardens, even a sketch, to determine our space and help us choose the plants we will grow. There are a few key questions to ask yourself to ensure that the time you spend planning your garden is as productive as possible.

How many plants can I grow in the space I have?

One of the most frequent mistakes of gardeners is to pile up too many crops in their gardens, which leads to overcrowding and poor harvests as the plants grow and compete for the best nutrients.

What is the best layout for my plants?

It is usually necessary to rearrange the plants on a plan until you get the perfect arrangement. For example, sprawling squash should be at the edge of vegetable beds to not suffocate other crops. On the other hand, leafy crops like summer lettuce can take advantage of the shade provided by taller plants, and plants like sweet corn should always be grown in blocks rather than in a single row so that they can reproduce correctly by the wind.

What do I need to buy or order?

It is essential to carefully plan orders for seeds and garden supplies so that you can start growing as soon as the weather permits.

When should I plant?

It is important to establish a calendar of the best times to plant each crop in your area. For best results, some crops such as tomatoes and peppers should be started under cover or indoors several weeks before your last frost. Other crops such as beans and squash cannot be sown until the outside temperatures are warm enough.

What could go wrong?

Think about what could be causing the problems. For example, large blocks of crops can easily be attacked by pests like aphids, so be sure to include flowering plants to attract beneficial insects to your plan, or a sudden heatwave could paralyze young people. Tender plants unless you have provided adequate irrigation or adequate shade.

All of this planning can be done with a pen and paper, but it can be time-consuming. It gets more and more complicated as more plants are grown, especially if you take into account several years of crop rotation plans.

CHAPTER TWO

Building a Raised Bed Gardening

The advantages of growing on raised beds are many; first of all, with this technique, it will be much easier to differentiate the soil according to the needs of the plant, compared to the classic cultivation on the ground.

By opting for this type of cultivation it will also be much more convenient and quick to work the soil and carry out all maintenance operations, it will be possible to drastically reduce the problem of weeds and, by avoiding compacting the soil with foot traffic, it will also allow a better flow of air and water to the roots of the plants.

Another important advantage is that by deciding to grow our vegetables, rather than aromatic herbs or flowering plants, using the raised bed technique, it will also be possible to do it on the balcony, on the terrace or perhaps in an area of the garden that was previously unused because it has no land with the right characteristics.

In essence, this cultivation technique consists of raising the land destined for the plants and delimiting the different crops through the creation of simple structures obtained by assembling wooden planks rather than bricks or stones of various kinds.

Gardening raised beds is a practice that was used long before colonial times. It has become increasingly popular among home gardeners because they can be installed in small inconvenient places of entry, it is a solution for gardening on land that can be installed almost anywhere in a limited period of time. They are also a perfect way to attach an appealing aspect to your yard and can bring other advantages as well as being a workplace than a dug garden.

The elevated beds are garden beds that are designed higher than the surrounding land. They are constructed no wider than four feet so that work in them is easy to reach. The length you want them to be can be any length. The distance is kept small, and there's no need to walk on the field to avoid compacting the soil.

The advantages of a raised bedside garden include easy access to the farm, better management of soil conditions and higher yields with less square footage. They are a good choice for construction in areas of poor soil like poor drainage or rocky areas.

This gardening method is much less difficult for disease and pest control. The soil structure will greatly benefit from the mulching and the accompanying planting and create a healthier plant that can defend itself against these problems. The addition of organic mulch will also improve the structure of the soil and feed the microorganisms living in the soil. These microorganisms are necessary to work the soil and add nutrients necessary for plants to thrive.

Raised garden beds are a wonderful idea. Depending on the size of the gardens, you can complete most of the weekends, create and plant a raised bed garden to blend in with your yards' natural environment, and attract wildlife, including birds and butterflies.

A safe and environmentally friendly way of gardening.

Organic gardening is in harmony with nature, away from gardening. A healthy and productive crop is produced so that both you and the environment are healthier.

How to Build a Raised Bed Gardening Step by Step

The contained lifted garden bed is one of the most common. Numerous vegetable and herbal gardens, as well as flower gardens, provide perfect growing conditions. Many fruits also do well in raised garden beds, including strawberries, grapes, and raspberries.

There are steps for a wooden upholstered bed as most elevated beds are made from wood.

Step One

Selecting a location is one of the most important decisions you make while building an elevated bed garden. Select a region that gets full sun, as most vegetables need full sun. If you want to plant vegetables that require partial sunlight, either build another bed in a different location or find a location that receives complete and partial sunlight. Also, make sure the area is flat, so water is easy, and all areas receive constant and equal amounts of water. If you want to make watering quick, consider installing a quick-to-use drip irrigation system to keep your garden watered.

Step Two

Decide your garden size and shape. Make sure you can reach all of your gardens without going into bed. Try to keep the garden long and narrow, allowing you to access all your vegetables without actually entering the garden. That's nice because the soil won't get compressed from running over it. This will give you carrots growing as straight as an arrow. Note accessibility is important, and if you want to place your garden against a fence, try to make it just 3 feet long so you don't have to walk into the garden. The depth of an elevated bed garden is up to you, but the deeper, the better, especially if you grow carrots or parsnips that need deeper soil. If you can, make your bed 12 inches tall!

Step Three

Your site's planning is very critical. Once you have your garden shape and scale, start building the bed. Grab the existing sod and loosen the soil below to a depth of eight to twelve inches. This gives your garden extra depth and good drainage. To move quickly, just cover the current sod and soil with newspaper or cardboard.

Step Four

Now it's time to build the bed. Using rot-resistant lumber like cedar or one of the newer composite woods to create your bed. Depending on the size of the garden, 'two by six' pieces of wood will create the entire garden. Cut the pieces to the appropriate length, add them to a simple frame. There are several different ways to add the wood, but choose one that is simple for you and can hold well for years of use.

Step Five

After building the frame in a spot, make sure you level your bed from all directions. This is a necessary move because if your bed is not level, you will find that water flows off one section of the garden and sits in another. If part of your frame is high, just remove any under it until you have a level frame.

Step Six

It's time to fill your garden with soil and compost after leveling. This will allow you to create a garden with great soil, ideal for growing vegetables. You can plant or sow seeds when they are full and raked.

Maintain a Raised Bed

The raised bed gives plants better protection against frost and pests than a flower bed because of its height. However, to avoid invasion or frost damage, some maintenance needs to be done.

The best way to manage aphids and cryptogamic diseases is by preventive steps. By properly combining plants, chemical plant protection products can be avoided. Certain varieties of flowers and vegetables release substances that are beneficial to other species through their leaves and roots. Chervil, then, is scaring snails and aphids. Plant species also each have specific requirements for nutrients. They are made more resistant by the combined crops and fertilizers.

You should create a protective fence around the edge of your flowerbed, to prevent snails from attacking your salads. A fine mesh screen, placed on the ground, protects your crops against voles. Special coatings reduce the risk of cryptogamic diseases, root and trunk rot, as well. The wooden beds have to be lined with a pool cover, as a precaution.

If you grow perennials or grow under a frame, you'll need a protective film, a winter veil, or a blanket to protect your bed from frost in winter. You can also shelter your plants there if you have a greenhouse.

Wash the soil layer from time to time using a rake and take advantage of this to remove weeds, to increase the quality of water and nutrients. Biodegradation causes the soil to sag over time, making it necessary to add a small amount of soil. Even if you regularly fertilize your flowerbed, after six years, you'll need to replace all the layers of soil. The humus layers are indeed exhausted after this time, and the draining layer no longer fulfills its role.

Advantages of Raised Bed Gardening

As already mentioned in the introduction, gardening is no longer limited to greenhouses or yard-houses. Today, you can quickly build an indoor beautiful and serene garden. Many people now use them for indoor gardening. These beds are suitable for fruit plants, flowers, and vegetables. Also, the height of the beds decreases the back pressure you get when dealing with traditional gardens with constant bending.

There are many advantages to gardening with raised beds. Most of them are here:

- Not only are raised beds easy to maintain, but they are also less prone to certain types of weeds. So, it avoids the unnecessary use of herbicides. Other than that, when the soil quality isn't very good, raised beds are ideal. Raised beds to allow you to control the soil quality, so you can plant different plant types using different soil qualities.
- The excess humidity is not retained when you plant flowers or vegetables. So the roots get a chance to breathe freely. This is especially useful when heavy showers are provided in the field, which tends to erode the soil. In this case, the water is fast draining away, and the soil is not eroding. So, you're not going to face a waterlogging crisis or ruined soil.

- Another benefit of this bed style is optimizing the available space. You can grow plants close to each other without overcrowding, which increases yields.

- As the soil is above the ground, it's going to warm up faster than a conventional flower bed. This warmth will help to improve and improve plant growth.

- Rising beds are ideal for seniors who want to indulge in gardening without putting undue strain on their backs. People with back problems are also benefited.

CHAPTER THREE

Types of Water Irrigation System

A garden needs water to grow well. Many people prefer a garden irrigation system to water it themselves. Most people think of only one option, which is the massive irrigation network used in large fields. These sprinklers are usually expensive and hard to install. They can also be complicated. The good news, however, is that smaller irrigation systems are available for personal gardens. They are user-friendly, energy- and water-efficient.

As you know, rainwater is planting water's best source. Modern irrigation system uses plant rainwater. It also minimizes your water and energy bill. Rainwater irrigation systems come with a timer, and you can program it as you like. These systems styles can be modified based on garden needs. Considering the garden layout, the sprinklers are mounted on that basis.

The sprinklers will be placed in the garden at regular intervals, using existing pipes. Installation requires linking pipework and adding water jets. It's so easy you can do it yourself. If you build yourself, it will dramatically reduce the cost.

Thousands of homeowners spend millions on water-irrigation systems each year. Watering your lawn by hand is neither fun nor effective. Plants and gardens need watering regularly. If you wait until it's time to rescue your plant from near-death then expect it to recover immediately, the plant will be put too much stress on. Too little water followed by too much water is an invitation to disease and other issues and is very bad for the plant's overall health.

The solution is being consistent, and the way forward is to establish a routine. Only shaking a hose and making the leaves wet doesn't put any water on the roots and is completely pointless, so you'll have to water the plant again the next day because the roots are dry. The number one best solution to this is to buy a long water wand attachment so that you can channel a large volume of water directly to the roots or where you want it to go at low pressure.

A general rule of thumb that differs because of the country where you live is that the average lawn requires about one inch of water a week. Place a few small rain gauges around your yard to make sure you're thorough and reliable. By using these gauges, you will know how effective your irrigation is and whether things need to be adjusted so that certain areas get less and others get more. Irrigating takes a lot of guesswork.

Deciding where the plants are located in an extremely critical and productive way of maintaining water in irrigation. Random planting is rather slow and adds even more work when you manually spray. You should have a plan for the laying out of your lawn before you begin the landscape. The best thing you can do is to create beds of similar plants, which will make maintenance and watering much easier.

Early in the morning, most experts found that watering your lawn or the garden was the most effective way. When you do so during the day's immediate heat, as much as 50%-60% may evaporate before it enters the dirt and is effective for the roots. The biggest tip I can't emphasize enough, if you are using an automatic water supply timer, is that you don't need to water the pelvis. A large deal of water can also be conserved.

Home irrigation is often done by a simple hose attached to the outside faucet of the home, but this is not the most cost-effective system for the owner as well as plant health. Instead, homeowners have many different options to use this ineffective method to water plants to water their lawn, garden or flowers. These systems can be used either on their own or in combination, depending on the landscape layout and the type of plants that need watering.

Hand Sprayers Irrigation

The most common ones are probably sprayers that attach to tubing and are used directly by hand in water plants. These are the most inefficient products for water plants and require the most effort. The cheapest and easiest to set up are, however. Aware consumers should also reduce the water expended on enhancing their inconveniences.

Sprinklers

For water lawns and plants, sprinklers may be used. They are available in a wide variety of styles and sizes so that they can be both the type of plants that are used and a specific landscape. These minimize the effort needed for water areas, although they still have the problem of spreading large amounts of water not used by crops. It is best used in large areas of grass.

Advantages of sprinkler irrigation

- It suits almost all types of soil;
- It can be adapted for different types of topography;
- It can be mobile or fixed;
- Uniform application in the plantation;
- It can be used together with fertigation;
- Low risk of soil erosion.

Disadvantages of sprinkler irrigation

- High implementation cost;
- Low efficiency in places with strong winds;
- Low effectiveness in places with high temperatures;
- Need for a clean source and free of water residues.

Drip Irrigation Systems.
These products use tube lengths in the garden on the next floor. When activated, they directly give the plant roots drops of water. These products are the most efficient watering method for plants and cost the least in water.

Often known as drop-by-drop irrigation. This type of irrigation is used in areas where water is scarce and significantly optimizes this resource. The operation idea is to distribute the water through drippers, which will moisturize the root zone of each plant.

There are several benefits to this irrigation system: it holds water well, it is well controlled, the water directly reaches every plant or crop, its installation is easy. It is simply a general tube diversified into small PVC pipes, with small mouths supplying water to each particular plant or crop.

You can also add timers or automatic systems, which will make the job much easier. It is a commonly used device as it mostly prevents the growth of mold or vegetation, apart from holding the moisture very well. It may cause the nozzles that water each plant to spoil after a long period of time, or because of bad weather conditions, but this is not a very common issue.

Greenhouse Irrigation

A combination of sprinklers and drip irrigation systems can completely water a whole greenhouse for greenhouse owners as well as increase the level of humidity within a greenhouse to improve plant health. These systems are fitted with hoses and feature miniature sprinklers that directly spray into specific pots.

Greenhouse irrigation systems are made up of different elements, which vary according to the needs and particularities of irrigation for each crop or farmer.

In greenhouses, plants are not irrigated from the water that comes from the atmosphere but must be watered by implementing an irrigation system if we want them to be well cultivated, which conserve humidity and growth.

First, it is important to analyze the conditions that these plants need and to decide which irrigation system is the one that will guarantee better results. These types of irrigation regulate air humidity and soil temperature.

Greenhouse watering systems come in many shapes, shapes, and sizes. One of the first things you need to remember when developing greenhouse watering systems is the demand you would need for the type of garden you water. Mind also that some plants may require more water and some less. With certain watering systems, you will be able to automate the watering needed for each plant, so one of the first things you need to do is to measure your needs. This phase is possibly the most critical in an automatic irrigation system of the sort.

Running water system

It is the irrigation system that can best adapt to each farmer's needs or the person who is going to install it. But this irrigation is the most common technique of collecting water from the middle barrels and PVC pipes.

One of the greatest advantages you see in this irrigation is that you save a lot of costs and a total ecological system.

CHAPTER FOUR

How to Make the Right Compost

Compost is a high-quality organic fertilizer. It benefits the soil's structure, increases the amount of organic matter, and provides nutrients, especially micronutrients such as nitrogen, potassium, and phosphorus. It contains all the nutrients for the healthy growth of plants and releases them slowly, which allows a continuous contribution. Its correct application favors improving gardening conditions and can perfectly substitute manure.

The decomposition of organic products forms the compost, which fertilizes the land. In addition, organic matter decomposes aerobically (with oxygen). This can be formed by different types of organic waste, such as the remains of fruits, vegetables, animal feces, leaves, eggshells and tea bags.

Compost is the result of the fermentation of organic or vegetable waste. To optimize the fermentation, it is essential to have a high humidity level and good ventilation of the compost.

Place your composter in a shaded place, and above all, do not make a "floor" or concrete screed below the composter. It is very important that the compost is in direct contact with the soil of your garden. Larvae, insects, earthworms, fungi, and bacteria will "nest" in the compost. They promote the ventilation of your compost, degrade waste, and improve the quality of your compost.

The compost is what remains after you have started a process of composting household. That is the process of decomposition and humification on residues of organic substances, such as the leaves of your garden, the grass cut from the lawn, etc.

Depending on the composting method that you have adopted, you will get a different type of compost, but basically, they can be categorized into three types:

- fresh compost
- ready compost
- ripe compost

The fresh compost (from 2 to 4 months in the case of composting with the heap) is still being transformed. Being still rich in nutrients, it is excellent as a fertilizer and for plant growth. Be careful, however, to apply it directly to the roots because this compost is still not very stable.

The compost ready (from 5 to 8 months), however, is stable, since the decomposition process does not produce more heat. On the other hand, it is less suitable for use as a fertilizer. We recommend using it in vegetable gardens or gardens as fertilizer before sowing or transplanting.

The mature compost (12/18 or 24 months) is the most stable one. Therefore, it is the least suitable as a fertilizer. However, it is perfect in direct contact with the roots or seeds and as potting soil for potted plants or even in the case of re-seeding and mowing of lawns.

Importance and benefits of compost

At some point, everyone can start working on the land or building gardens inside our homes. If we started planting the bean seeds as children in kindergarten, or already out of necessity.

But something that is highly needed to help nutritiously and healthily grow what we sow is compost. Also known as organic fertilizer that helps the plants grow well.

It is a scientific fact that organic matter is an extremely significant soil fertility element. This helps to considerably enhance the earth's stability and properties, both physical and chemical.

Compost is an element by itself which can be formed naturally with the materials provided by the earth. If they are very much of animal or vegetable matter, they return to earth at the end of their life cycle.

We may help generate it in the same way that it is created naturally by recycling the waste in our homes. This will help boost the plants' health and growth, so they will get better nutrients for them.

Compost use helps improve soil efficiency by reducing abrupt temperature changes. Additionally, fertilizer use is also very detrimental to soil, and compost substitutes for soil-affecting chemicals.

The garbage that is collected in our homes has as its final destination the dumps of the cities. Places that are sources of infection and that can cause a lot of damage to the skin, eyes and respiratory tract.

It is very important to create awareness in our communities regarding the contamination produced by garbage. That is why we share five beneficial aspects of composting in our homes and parks.

- It returns nutrients to the soil, controls erosion and prevents soil wear caused by rain washing.
- It corrects the structure of the soils and acts as a sponge that retains water, which gradually releases to the benefit of the plants.
- It retains moisture and allows air to pass through.
- Recycle and reduce the amount of organic waste, to convert it into compost.
- It serves as an antibiotic against microorganisms.

If we reduce the production of waste in our home, we could positively impact the total balance of pollution. Therefore, we all have the task of making our own habitat a safe and clean place.

How to make compost

Making compost, or composting doesn't just mean building and keeping a compost bin in order. It also means knowing and controlling what you're pouring into it to get a good fertilizer. This book will give you simple guidelines on what you should be doing and what you should not be putting into compost. Follow the three "Rs" (Reduce, Reuse and Recycle) to reduce the amount of waste that needs to be thrown away!

We said that by compost, we mean the product of the decomposition, accelerated and controlled by man, of organic substances. Among these, kitchen scraps. Mainly vegetable remains fruit peels, coffee and tea grounds, eggshells, fireplace ash, etc.

But also gardening. For example, pruning branches, mowing of lawns, dry leaves, withered flowers, garden waste.

The advantages of compost

Home composting offers several advantages.

First of all, it guarantees the correct closure of the waste cycle, given that the workforce makes up about a third of the total amount of household waste. The compost DIY avoids landfill or to ' incinerator, thereby reducing disposal costs. At the end of the home composting procedure, then we will have a natural organic fertilizer available.

This will be usable in the vegetable garden, in the garden, or for potted plants instead of chemical fertilizer pollutants. We will thus save money by limiting the purchase of potting soil, substrates, and organic fertilizers. And at the same time, we will reduce the atmospheric pollution produced by the combustion of these waste, also avoiding the infiltration of leachate into the soil.

The compost, such as natural organic fertilizer, gradually releases into the soil the elements indispensable for the growth of the plant, such as nitrogen, phosphorus, potassium, and trace elements.

What can become compost and what cannot

Anyone wishing to proceed to home composting must first of all pay attention to what to put in the composter.

The kitchen and gardening wastes indicated above, as well as other biodegradable materials, are doing well. These include uncoated paper, cardboard, sawdust, and shavings from untreated wood.

Attention, all glass, plastic, and metal objects, synthetic fabrics, chemicals, expired drugs, coated paper, and litters of dogs and cats must be absolutely avoided.

With great caution, leftovers of food of animal origin and foods cooked in small quantities can also be added. Same warning for leaves of plants resistant to degradation (magnolia, beech, chestnut, conifer needles, etc.).

How to make compost: cumulative composting

We now come to the various forms of composting. The most widespread is certainly the cumulative one. Here we will have to choose places that are practicable all year round and located below trees that lose their leaves in winter. In winter, we must allow solar radiation, while in summer, the sunlight must be mitigated. Placing chopped wood under the pile (10-15 cm) is another good practice to avoid mud formation in the winter months.

The minimum height of the pile must be 50-60 cm in order to retain heat and guarantee microbial activity. However, the 1.3-1.5 meters must not be exceeded. Otherwise, the material risks compacting under its weight.

The best form in the summer is the trapeze shape. It allows you to adequately absorb rain and replace evaporated water. In winter, on the contrary, it is good practice to use the triangular one, to avoid the excessive accumulation of rain inside the pile, given the poorer evaporation.

The secrets to making a good compost

The secret to successful composting is in the correct mixing of the waste. This activity is essential to allow the right activity of microorganisms and avoid the onset of putrefaction phenomena, with the consequent bad smells.

In practice, it is necessary to create a correct stratification, alternating the most humid and nitrogen waste (grass clippings and kitchen residues), with the drier and more carbonaceous ones (shredded branches, broken cardboard, wood chips, dry leaves, straw, etc.).), which guarantee good porosity and the correct supply of oxygen to the pile. The initial water content must be between 45 and 65%, while as regards the right nitrogen-carbon ratio, it is good to know that for each gram of the first one, you need 20 or 30 of the second.

To ensure the correct supply of humidity, the pile can be covered during rainy periods with materials such as "non-woven" or jute sheets or layers of leaves and straw of 5-10 cm. In this way, we will be able to retain water without compromising air circulation. The cover can also be useful to protect from excessive drying during the summer months.

Another aspect that should not be underestimated for the success of composting is the right oxygenation. It is essential for bacteria that perform aerobic biodegradation. For a correct exchange of air, it is, therefore, necessary not to compress the material of the pile and turn it periodically with a pitchfork, an operation to be repeated frequently if the cluster is not very porous.

How to make compost: the fertilizer

An alternative to cumulation can be the manure. It consists of a hole dug in the ground where to accumulate organic waste. In this case, however, problems may arise due to the tendency to accumulate too much water, especially in the case of the waterproofed substrate.

Another typical problem is the insufficient exchange of oxygen with the outside by the materials deposited on the bottom.

Those who choose this system will, therefore, have to take some precautions. Among these, the insertion of drainage pipes, a layer of gravel, or a pallet under the organic material placed in the hole.

The same pallets can also be used to separate the waste from the hole wall, in order to guarantee a good exchange of air.

How to make compost using the composter

As can be guessed, the heap is particularly suitable for those who live in houses with large gardens that produce large quantities of twigs and green waste. The composter made of plastic, wood or network instead is more useful for those citizens who are gardens of small and medium-size, originating less waste.

They are containers of variable volumes (from 200 to 1,000 liters), with various types of openings. Their use allows limiting the visual impact of decomposing materials, ensuring their sanitation and less affected by atmospheric conditions. However, there may be difficulties in turning the material over if they cannot be opened on one side. If you intend to purchase a plastic composter, prefer those that have systems that promote air circulation in the internal walls.

But how does a composter work?

The operation of these tools is very simple. After having sorted, simply insert a layer of coarse twigs at its base, then alternately adding layers of nitrogen and carbonaceous waste, according to the same principle analyzed previously. After 3-4 months, the vegetable waste must be turned over and then put back into the composter.

After a period of 5-6 months, the lower part of the waste, brown in color and similar to the humus of the undergrowth, will have produced a homogeneous compost that is already available for use. This fraction must, therefore, be sieved and left to dry in the sun for a few days. The wood waste not yet transformed must instead be reintroduced into the composter.

Of course, the use of these do-it-yourself tools implies the same adoption of good practices as for cumulation. First of all, it is necessary to ensure proper mixing by alternating nitrogen and carbon layers. Then it is necessary to ensure good air circulation by inserting coarse twigs and turning the material once every six months. Finally, it is necessary to maintain optimal humidity (55-60%), which favors the reproduction of aerobic microorganisms.

Generally, compost is ready after about 12-20 weeks in winter and 10-15 in summer. The completion of its degradation is evident both from the appearance and form the characteristic smell.

CHAPTER FIVE

The Right Vegetables Month by Month

Growing your own vegetables is a very fun pastime, which also has many beneficial benefits such as healthy food (you know what additives were used if any), exercise, outdoor work etc. Growing your own vegetables is also a wonderful activity for the entire family to participate, as it helps kids understand better how nature works and where food comes from.

Some people think a lot of space is needed to grow your own vegetables. When you are trying to provide the family with a range of vegetables every day of the year, this is definitely real. It's not true if you cultivate your own vegetables to complement your grocery shopping to have some fresh vegetables. For example, four or so runner bean (Pole Bean) plants in a patio container should provide more than enough beans for a family of four for a few months.

When it comes to vegetables, each country in the world has different varieties that grow best in their specific climate, even in some countries a specific crop that grows well in one region does not grow at all in another as the climate and atmosphere are different. It's here where some of the fun comes into growing your own because you can experiment with different vegetable varieties from different parts of the world to see what you can and can't produce, experimentation will also be required to establish specific growing conditions for these unique varieties for your environment.

There are two ways to have our own gardens at home, in the external area (backyard) or in the internal area (kitchen, balcony, balcony, service area). Let's deal with the first way, which will probably be subject to the weather. The success of a vegetable garden, in this case, is directly related to the right moment of each planting of herbs, vegetables, and vegetables. Each month has its characteristics, which make them more suitable for each species.

The plants are different from each other in relation to the type of soil and temperatures necessary for their full development, so it is very important to know what are the most suitable options for each season of the year.

Below, we have prepared a list of the most used plants in vegetable gardens and which month, or months, are most suitable for planting.

- **January:** lettuce, watercress, celery, various cabbages, radish, almond, turnip, beet, arugula, chicory, spinach, sweet potato, parsley, coriander, purslane, carrot, Brussels sprouts, and cabbage;

- **February:** watercress, lettuce, chicory, beans, parsley, radish, cabbage, beets, cabbage, peas, spinach, and beans;
- **March:** carrot, almond, parsley, garlic, lettuce, chicory, spinach, celery, miscellaneous cabbages, cauliflower, broccoli, cabbage, watercress, celery, onion, coriander, peas, beans, beans, strawberry, turnip, radish, and cabbage ;
- **April:** watercress, almond, beet, turnip, parsley, garlic, arugula, chicory, celery, cauliflower, broccoli, cabbage, spinach, carrot, coriander, pea, asparagus, broad bean, lentil, strawberry, radish, lettuce, onion, and various cabbages;
- **May:** radish, carrot, almond, turnip, beet, arugula, parsley, chicory, celery, spinach, cauliflower, broccoli, winter cabbage, garlic, lettuce, potato, onion, various cabbages, fava, and strawberry;
- **June:** almond, carrot, turnip, beet, arugula, garlic, chicory, watercress, cauliflower, broccoli and winter cabbage;
- **July:** pea, almond, arugula, garlic, lettuce, radish, chicory, beet, broad bean, and cabbage;
- **August:** artichoke, white celery, jiló, eggplant, various peppers, peppers, tomatoes, onion, cabbage, asparagus, strawberry, melon, watermelon, and cucumber;

- **September:** lettuce, radish, beet, carrot, miscellaneous cabbages, cauliflower, broccoli, jiló, eggplant, miscellaneous peppers, peppers, tomatoes, squash, zucchini, green beans, cucumber, gherkin, parsley, coriander, onion, peas, spinach, fava beans, lentils, melons, watermelons, and turnips;

- **October:** chard, carrot, various cabbages, cauliflower, broccoli, cabbage, various peppers, peppers, tomatoes, eggplant, jiló, pumpkin, zucchini, green beans, cucumber, gherkin, *mandioquinha*, parsley, potato, sweet potato, coriander, watercress, lettuce, beet, broccoli, chicory, cumin, broad bean, melon, watermelon, turnip, radish, thyme, onion, and tomato;

- **November:** pumpkin, watercress, lettuce, radish, carrot, broccoli, cabbage, various cabbages, cauliflower, sweet potato, coriander, beet, spinach, beans, melon, watermelon, turnip, cucumber, and various peppers;

- **December:** pumpkin, zucchini, green beans, cucumber, carrots, cabbage, watercress, lettuce, beets, broccoli, various cabbages, spinach, melon, watermelon, turnip, various peppers, and radish.

There are still many herbs that are considered perennial, produce all year round, such as sage, parsley, chives, marjoram, basil, for example, but that cannot resist very low temperatures or frosts, so it is interesting that they are planted in more protected places.

Another important point to note is the use of greenhouses; for example, some plants in greenhouses have their productivity extended for many more months.

The other option, mentioned above, of growing a vegetable garden indoors is ideal for those who live in apartments and dream of having an organic garden without pesticides. This can be done in pots and the location chosen for its location inside the house, allows you to decide less for the month of the year and more for the climate that we create in the indoor environment.

You can create light and temperature conditions for your favorite herbs. We have selected some garden options available for sale that can give you a good idea of how to build yours. They can stay in the kitchen, laundry area, on the balcony, in short, wherever there is space available for you to cultivate your new hobby.

CHAPTER SIX

Growing Herbs

The practice of growing herbs has been around for many thousands of years, and both medical and culinary uses for these herbs have taken place. Herbs give us fragrances and tastes in these modern days, and they are also a very important part of your kitchen garden.

The great thing about herbs is that you don't have a lot of lands to grow, and, really, a small plot will make several applications for you, and all your herbs for your personal use would be easy to grow.

Another endearing thing about growing herbs is that they are very easy to cultivate, and even people who have never grown anything before will have no problem raising herbs in their home gardens.

The best time to plant the herbs is during the spring months, and a wonderful herb garden can also be built in your home, which is attractive and helps to grow ample numbers of herbs. A formal herb garden includes the use of traditional growing techniques, many of which have originated from the ages. A knot garden, for example, lets you grow herbs that boast knotty designs, and this type of growth has been practiced since the Middle Ages.

You can also seed part of a flower garden or even a vegetable garden to plant the seeds when you do not have a lot of space for growing herbs. In particular, as this helps to create a wonderful curvature for each floral or vegetable garden, you might wish to grow creeping rosemary and thyme.

The difference between perennial and annual herbs is also significant. The former type can grow year after year and can be incorporated into your herb garden's basic structure. Annuals, on the other hand, must be cleared before the freeze begins to kill them and be snipped during the summer seasons.

Basil is an outstanding example of an annual herb and an essential part of many foods in the Mediterranean. It can easily be planted after its seeds are harvested, but you need to plant seedlings if you want to bloom in summer.

Why grow herbs?

Did you ever buy fresh herbs specifically for a recipe you 're about to make at the grocery store? I did. This is an expensive buy, despite the number of herbs that are normally included. They also appear to degrade rapidly, unless careful care is taken to avoid damage.

Then why not go for dry herbs? Well, the fact is nothing beats the fresh kind of thing. Fresh herbs are more aromatic and have more flavor. Having an indoor or outdoor herb garden helps you to easily pick the herbs you need every day and make your home-made meals even more delicious.

Herbs can also have an ever-growing medicine cabinet or a ready-made supply of tea for you. They're also loved by pollinators, including bees and butterflies, which means the other plants will be healthier.

What do you need

To start with an herb garden, you need a few basics.

- Ground

Whether you plan indoors or outdoors, it doesn't matter, you'll need one, and you'll need a place to plant. That can be a number, a bed or containers raised up. You have an option, but be sure to check out the Common Errors section below for guidance on choosing your plants' best growing container.

Most herbs prefer conventional garden soil, but some Mediterranean plants need sandy soil well-drained. That includes the lavender, rosemary and berry. Check what your plants like, and group them together. For example, in a portion of your garden, you can add a small amount of sand to the garden soil for plants like dry plants. You may create a richer mix for those in another region who need more humidity.

Location, location, location

Most herbs love the sun, so pick a spot to get a generous amount of sun every day. Sunshine is important for healthy development, for at least 6 hours. However, the optimal location can vary, depending on the plant.

Some herbs like it dry, while others prefer a little bit of shade. For details that can help you pick the right location, you can check a seed packet, sticker, or mark on the pot (if you purchased your plant from a nursery)

You can mix tall plants that like to enjoy the sun with short plants that prefer some shade, with a little preparation. A giant parsley plant, for example, may provide shade for low-growing sweet grass.

A significant factor to remember when choosing a location is the distance between that location and your house. Can you face a rainstorm and get some chives for your early jamming? Would you care to stroll to the edge of your garden in search of a basil leaf while dinner is awaiting you?

Some people do not care a thing, but some may prefer to have their own herb garden nearby. Whatever you do, make sure it is easily available so you can keep a close eye on it and constantly harvest an endless supply of delicious spices and medicine.

Start your herb garden

It takes planning to create a good herb garden. Decide whether you want plants to grow in containers or in the field and whether you want to grow indoors, outdoors or both. You will also have to determine whether you want to continue using purchased seeds or plants.

Start the herbs inside

Do you have herb seeds to continue inside? You can choose to start planting and choose the "route from scratch," but for beginners, I don't recommend it. The rationale? Many seeds from herbs take a long time to germinate. Starting to grow annual plants and seeing them die in winter is also painful. Head into your nearest kindergarten to search for herbs available.

Plant herbs outside

When you've determined what you're planting, what kind of soil you need, and where to plant it, it's time to start. I like to make a diagram of my landscape, and then plan the grasses I want to put and where taking the height and width of the plants into account.

Instead, it depends on the herbs. In your current soil blend, garden dirt, sand, and/or moss. It is then time to dig. Dig a hole twice the size of your plant's root ball, remove the plant from the pot and loosen the roots. Place the plant in the pit and soil backfill.

Donate plenty of water to the farm. I always think it helps to mark my plants with a clear label on stakes. Often the difference between young plants is difficult to say, so a label makes all the difference.

If they are perennial, the herbs should be planted in the spring, but during the growing season, you can plant annuals almost anytime. I like planting annuals like cilantro regularly every few weeks, so my supply is constant throughout the year.

Container gardening

You may also grow the herbs outdoors or indoors in containers. If you need to, it's a perfect way to make sure you can push your plants around, and it can help prevent weeds like mint.

When selecting the container process, be sure to use a container that is wide and deep enough for your mature grass and has plenty of holes at the bottom to allow water to drain out. Put plenty of rocks or pottery pieces in the bottom, so drainage is possible.

For arid herbs, fill the container with compost or sand compost. Plant your grass, and soak it.

Caring for your herb garden

The rules are straight forward. Herbs mimic any other herb. They need to grow on light, water, and nutrients. When it comes to herbs, there's no special trick. Harvest by gathering or cutting the leaves, as required. Watch for weeds and look out for possible pests before they get into your garden so you can easily get rid of them in the event of an attack.

While herbs in your garden are no harder to grow than tomato plants in your vegetable patch or roses, the problem is that many people prefer to plant different herbs together and treat them as one and the same thing. For this reason, it is so important to decide what your plants like before they are planted together in the soil.

This also refers to providing the plants with nutrients. Be sure to remember your plants prefer the amount of fertilizer and don't assume all herbs want the same amount.

Herbs For You To Grow in Your Garden

Basil - It is the most frequently cultivated herb and is well known to herbal garden enthusiasts worldwide. The herb Basil grows well in low humidity and moist soil climes. Spring is the ideal season to start growing the Basil plant, but only after all frost risks have been alleviated as this plant is extremely susceptible to cold temperatures and can be harmed if exposed.

It is important to note when planting Basil that each plant is approximately twelve inches apart. This allows the growing plant to access sufficient water and makes it a healthy plant. After the planting of Basil, the development of mature leaves ready for harvest takes around six weeks. When the harvest is carried out, a proper drying method can lead to a savory dried plant, which can be used in a variety of recipes to delight your taste buds. In warm summer months, this robust herb would have grown to about one or two feet high and sprouting deep green or even pure leaves with tiny, white flowers.

Dill - Nothing could be easier than to cultivate the delicious Dill herb. Just a dispersion of grains thrown into your grassy garden will lead to stalks that can grow to four feet. The herbal set adds beauty and is used in many recipes. Dills Stalks have distinctive blue-green leaves, feathery and with striking yellow flowers.

The dill plant is a sun-loving plant that ensures a flourishing plant in areas with full exposure to sunlight. The best method to ensure a strong crop is an 8-10 inches gap between plants. You will go back about two weeks after sowing the seeds when the herbs exceed 1 inch in height and thin the area around each herb. This cycle ensures that each plant receives the necessary nutrient content from the soil and ensures that each plant is adequately exposed to sunlight.

Lavender - One of Lavender's most natural, fragrant herbs. This aromatic plant is a wonderful covering for any herb or flower garden because it grows delicate pink and purple flowers on high stalks. Lavender is a perennial plant, and in the middle of summer, it is at its best. Lavender is also an essential ingredient in aromatherapy, soap making and potpourri.

Although this hardy herb is easy to grow if choosing to start from seed form can require some extra work. The best way to implement this plant from your local gardening center is through fresh plants or root cuttings. These plants grow well in warm, alkaline-rich soil that is not water-logged. As the winter months close, the elegance of these plants will disappear, but in the next seasons, these plants will return stronger and lusher than last.

CHAPTER SEVEN

Growing fruit

Growing fruit trees and fruiting shrubs is an operation that our vegetable greenhouse, greenhouse or balcony, whether small or huge, will never lack.

The juicy and tasty fruit is the perfect complement to the nutritious vegetables and aromatic herbs offered to us by our garden.

Also, if we're not thinking about a real orchard, two rows of strawberries and a currant plant in a small vegetable garden or greenhouse would suffice to give us some vitamin-rich dessert. The round bushes of wild strawberries may also be planted at the edges of a flowerbed, where they will act as a decorative frame for our vegetable garden or greenhouse as well as being an enticing treat to taste when walking.

On the other side, if we have more room available, we can grow a small fruit tree plantation, choosing the trees that best match the environment, height, sun exposure, and soil type in our garden.

The fruit trees, which remind us of the Garden of Eden's romantic pictures, cheer up our garden and balcony's green space and give us a beauty that is always different depending on the season but never banal. From the beautiful spring flowers to the lush and green foliage rich in summer fruits to the mystical autumn colors and the romantic and enigmatic winter forms.

So only a tiny fruit tree on the balcony will help us rediscover the sight and sense of wonder for the everyday wonders that we are sadly sometimes unable to see any more today. Having fruit trees in the garden or on the balcony is also a way to have always available seasonal fruits and vegetables, suitable for the preparation of fresh and nutritious extracts and juices.

Here is a selection of some fruit trees to be planted in the garden, in the vegetable garden or on the balcony, to be chosen according to our preferences, the climatic conditions of the place where we live and depending on the room we have available.

1) Appletree

The apple tree is part of the fruit of Pome, to which all the fruit trees belong, the pulp of which contains a core of small seed. The apple tree can be grown in a large or medium-sized garden as well as in small vegetable gardens, where spindle bushes are probably more suitable. There are manyl varieties of apple trees that adopt various stages of harvesting and maturing, and grow fruits with different flavors. The apples have many characteristics and are suggested for various sweet and savory recipes.

Growing tips

In humus-rich, very loamy soils, the apple tree grows especially well. Having a healthy humidity in the soil and a humid environment is very critical. Planting an apple tree on dry or southern slopes is not advisable, and while the apple tree is not an especially fragile fruit tree, it is best to select the right variety for the area we live in. The Golden Delicious variety grows well in mild climate areas, while Geheimrat Oldenburg and James Grieve will yield good harvests in harsh climate zones.

Also, the apple tree is a fruit tree that can never survive in isolation but needs a pollinating insect that fertilizes its seeds, including bees. Since most varieties are incompatible with each other, i.e., they can not pollinate themselves, and it is important to plant different varieties nearby. Excellent pollinating varieties and varieties are among the most popular crops that complement each other harmoniously, for example, Golden Delicious and Granny Smith. The apple tree is a plant that horizontally grows its roots, and most of the roots that accumulate nutrients are in the upper layer of the soil. For this reason, the area under the canopy, which will be periodically supplied with natural fertilizer and compost, is very important to take good care of.

Some of the most common and easy to grow varieties:

- **Clara:** slightly acid fruit with acid pulp. It contains about 15 mg of vitamin C on 100 grams of pulp. It should be harvested in July and eaten fresh.

- **Gravenstein:** tasty, sweet fruit with juicy pulp. It contains about 8 mg of vitamin C on 100 grams of pulp. It should be harvested from mid-August to mid-September and consumed until December.

- **James Grieve:** tasty fruit, sweet and with juicy pulp. It contains about 7 mg of vitamin C on 100 grams of pulp. It should be harvested from mid-September to mid-October and consumed up to the end of November.

- **Geheimrat Oldenburg:** fruit with an almost neutral flavor with juicy pulp. It contains about 1 mg of vitamin C on 100 grams of pulp. It should be harvested in September and consumed up to the end of December.

- **Goldparmane:** fruit with a sweet taste and crunchy pulp. It contains about 18 mg of vitamin C on 100 grams of pulp. It should be harvested from mid-September to mid-October and consumed from November to February.

- **Cox Orange:** fruit with a sweet and delicate flavor, with very juicy pulp. It contains up to 20 mg of vitamin C on 100 grams of pulp. It should be harvested in October and consumed until February.

- **Golden Delicious:** sweet and tasty fruit, the particular aroma of wine, tender and juicy pulp. It contains about 8 mg of vitamin C on 100 grams of pulp. It should be harvested from mid-October to mid-November and consumed from January to April.

- **Granny Smith:** fruit with green skin and a sour taste, with a crunchy and juicy pulp. It contains about 16 mg of vitamin C on 100 grams of pulp. It should be harvested in October and consumed until the end of February.

2) Peartree

The pear is a fruit tree belonging to the family of the Rosaceae and whose roots are not entirely understood, even though it is considered to be native to Asia. The spindle-shaped bush is particularly suitable for small family gardens, while you can choose medium or tall trees for medium-large gardens. The pear has rich properties and is ideal for many sweet and savory recipes. Pears are also commonly used in cooking for the preparation of centrifuges and extracts of fruits and vegetables.

Growing tips

The pear tree is a fruit tree that prefers a warm climate, has deep roots, and extends horizontally, so it needs deeper soil than the apple tree. The pear tree reacts to stagnant groundwater negatively and loves nutrient-rich, warm, rather light soils. Pear grows well, especially in a sunny position and needs the right partner for pollination, just like apple trees.

Some of the easier to grow varieties:

- Angelica: fresh and aromatic fruit with a juicy pulp. The fruit is harvested from late August to early September and is harvested from the second half of September. This plant variety is particularly suitable for hill areas.
- Williams Christ: sweet and juicy fruit with very tender pulp. The fruit is harvested from mid-August to late September and ripens until the end of October. To be well cultivated, this variety of plant needs a well-sheltered position.
- Good Luisa d'Avranches: sweet and juicy fruit, which is harvested in September and ripens until the end of October. This particular variety is suitable for cultivation only in warm areas.
- Favorita di Clapp: delicately acidic fruit with a juicy pulp, which is harvested from mid-August to mid-September

and ripens until mid-October. This variety of plant is very vigorous and suitable for medium-altitude positions

- Beurrè Rocca: juicy and sugary fruit with a semi-fine pulp that is harvested from late August to mid-September and ripens until the end of October
- Conference: fruit with a sweet and delicate flavor and juicy and grainy pulp. The fruit is harvested from mid-September to mid-October and ripens until early December.
- Thigh: juicy and sugary fruit, which collects and ripens in July. This variety is suitable for very hot climates
- Spina Carpi: slightly acidic fruit with a juicy pulp that is harvested from late September to late October and ripens until late December. This variety is suitable for cool and windy hilly areas.
- Volpina: fruit with a slightly sour aroma and firm pulp, which is harvested in early October and ripens until the end of November. This variety is suitable for hill areas.

3) Quince Apple

The quince is a family Rosaceae plant, which develops in a tiny tree whose height does not exceed 4-5 meters. The quince is an ancient tree that has not undergone man-made modifications or grafts and is, in all probability, the tree that was present in Eden 's garden. Quinces are poorly cultivated today, but quince plants are often inserted as rootstocks for pear and apple trees into orchards. Quinces have to be prepared to eat and are used in many national dishes' recipes. Quince is often grown as a shrub because it remains smaller in size, making growing and care easier.

Growing tips

The quince needed a lot of light and a not too heavy soil to grow. Unlike pears and apple trees, the quince is self-fertilizing, and only a single specimen can be found. Quince can also be grown in containers, and it spreads a good fragrance if held in the winter living room.

Some of the most common and easy to grow varieties:

- Champion: large and very fragrant fruits
- Meliform: large fruits and very abundant harvest
- Van Deman: fruit with excellent pulp flavor
- Kostantinopoler: a frost-resistant plant with large fruits

4) Cherry

The cherry belongs to the family of stone fruits, to which the fruit trees belong whose pulp contains a hard-shelled kernel that protects the seed. Both tall and fruit are the most common varieties of cherry only after 6-8 years. They are also not recommended for those who have a small vegetable garden or greenhouse, even because of the size of their leaves.

Growing tips

The cherry requires a dark, smooth, silky soil and not too moist to grow. It doesn't need special attention, if not the position: it must be put in full light. Since the cherry isn't self-fertilizing, at least two adjacent specimens must always be planted.

Some of the most common and easy to grow varieties:

- Durone di Vignola and Durone della Marca: hard-pulp fruits
- Precocchio della Marca e Goriziana: soft pulp fruits
- Bigarreau Napoleon and Bigarreau Moreau: semi-hard fruit

5) Marasco

The Prunus Cerasus, commonly known as Amareno or Marasco, is a Rosaceae family fruit tree whose fruit, black cherry, is one of the most delicious in our garden that we can find. There are also shrub-shaped with smaller dimensions, suitable for growing in the vegetable garden or in the greenhouse, but their fruits will be more acidic than larger trees. The best and easiest variety to grow is the Schattenmorelle, whose fruit is dark red in color and has a more acidic taste, while if you prefer a sweeter and juicier fruit, you will have to select the newer Morellenfeuer variety, which is well suited to all types of terrains.

Growing tips

Amarasco is a self-fertile species, so just plant one. These fruit trees grow well on all soils and become sick only when they are planted in hot, humid soil. We'll need to grow our fruit tree in a sunny position to have sweet and juicy black cherries. For a year, the amarasco fruit on the tree, which is why it is important to prune the branches periodically before a new jet is attacked to create an abundance of fruit annually.

6) Peach

The peach tree is a fruit tree that belongs to the family Rosaceae, originally from the Middle East. It is typically grown in its shrub-shaped form, ideal to be kept in the balcony, vegetable garden or flower pots. The most popular and easiest cultivable varieties are:

- Michelini: white, very aromatic, late flowering and less prone to frost
- Sant'Anna: scented pulp and excellent flavor
- Ceccarelli quince: yellow, aromatic and with an abundant harvest

Growing tips

The peach tree grows especially well in mild climate areas, as it requires a lot of heat and humus-rich soil. Avoid growing it in areas that are too cold and hot, unless it is in a specially protected area. Late frosts also threaten peach trees as they bloom in early spring (March-April). Peaches bear fruit for a year as well as amareno, and must, therefore, be pruned annually.

7) Apricot

The apricot is a fruit tree of uncertain origin, and some sources suggest that this tree would come from China, while others trace it back to Persia or Armenia. The apricot is a medium-sized plant, as it never goes beyond 5-7 meters in height, suitable for growing in your garden or in a small or medium-sized garden.

The most common and easiest varieties to grow are:

- Della Val Venosta: particularly suitable for cold areas, fragrant pulp and delicate flavor
- Nancy apricot: ancient French variety, abundant harvest with frost-sensitive flowers
- Reale d'Imola: sweet and fragrant pulp, easy to grow

Growing tips

In terms of climate, apricot trees are much more demanding than peaches: they generally grow well with mild temperatures and in a dry, clean, and nutrient-rich soil. These fruit trees are also vulnerable to the possibility of late frosts, such as peach trees. Many of the key dangers for this plant's proper growth is represented by strong winds, which, in particular, may cause very serious damage to bloom.

8) Lemon

Lemon is a fruit tree native to India and Indochina. This plant tolerates pot cultivation well because, in nature, it is a low-sized tree with vigorous but slow growth.

Growing tips

Lemon is a fruit tree that we can keep healthy in the garden or on the balcony, even in pots. However, to make it grow well, it is important to have a pot of the right size (the plant's foliage must be contained within the diameter of the pot), a porous, organic and draining soil (we suggest using material at the bottom of the pot which facilitates the water flow and prevents stagnation) and remember to repot at the beginning of the spring every two years. The lemon plant should be sheltered during the winter in warm and sunny surroundings with a minimum temperature of 13 degrees.

The most common and easy to grow varieties are:

- *Femminello comune*: the most common cultivar in Italy, it has medium vigor, and the fruit produces an abundant, clear and very aromatic juice.
- *Femminello syracusano*: this type of lemon is a plant of great vigor, with rapid growth and which bears fruit earlier than other Mediterranean lemons.
- *Femminello Apireno Continella*: compared to the common Femminello, it has the advantage of not having

seeds but, on the other hand, has an excessively thick skin, the plant is thorny, and the fruits are small.

- *Monachello*: this is the Italian cultivar that absolutely resists badly dry, a fungal disease very common in fruit trees, especially citrus fruits.

Some people enjoy growing vegetables in their garden, and if you're among those who want to grow vegetables in the garden, then using vegetable seeds and some useful techniques, you can easily grow your own vegetables in your backyard or greenhouse.

Many nursery shops hold Veg Seed varieties in their store; you can select the one that needs different efforts and grows in less time. Some of the Vegetable Seeds are cumin seeds, also referred to as jeera. It is warm and sharp in taste, and its scent persists for a long time in the food as it brings a different taste and flavors to the food. Cowpea-Kokand and sadabahar, these crop types can be grown during the season, and it takes about 45 to

50 days to germinate. It is medium-height grass. Brinjal seeds are used to grow a high variety of brinjals and take 75 to 80 days to harvest.

Consider buying pesticides, insecticides and fertilizers after selecting vegetables. Pesticides and insecticides avoid soil and pest. Tomato feed is a strong soil fertilizer if you enjoy growing fruits like strawberries after harvesting. Tomato is a growing vegetable grown by most in their garden.

If you're new to agriculture, it's suggested to help any experts or someone who has experience growing vegetables at home as experts can provide some valuable tips on growing vegetables. They can also facilitate you figure out your farming-related questions. Farming isn't as hard as it seems, although it requires effort and time.

If you have less room or space at home or a small garden area, you can prefer growing vegetables in pots and containers. Most people live in apartments and multi-story houses with no garden area. They can grow vegetables in containers and pots. It is also economical since less money is spent on food.

Any individual can grow the vegetables in their garden, though they need some expert advice. Just by growing vegetables in your home, you can provide a balanced diet for your family and children. This helps kids adapt to eating healthy, nutritious food.

Why is it important to grow your own vegetables?

Whether it's a balcony, a terrace or a real field, almost always there's something for gardening! So why not combine pleasure with a little patch of vegetables? Compelling reasons for growing your own fruits and vegetables!

1 - Gardening is good for your health

A safe mind in a sound body! The exercise and the efforts it brings to gardening do you good. All the studies on the relationships between vegetation and living environment show the undeniable benefits of greenery's presence on our well-being! The daily gardening practice stimulates both the mental and the physical. In short, taking care of the plants and your garden means taking care of yourself!

2 - Know what you are eating

It's our responsibility to eat well, and this responsibility is accentuated when we have kids we can only hope for the best. When we grow our own fruits and vegetables, we at least know what we eat! When you have children, it helps them realize that the source of food is not only the temples of consumption that are supermarkets but also in the vegetable field.

3 - Save money

Even with a small garden, it is several hundred euros less to spend in stores. Rodolphe Grosleziat claims to save the value of around three times the minimum wage by buying almost no fruit and vegetables anymore! To find out more, discover its anti-crisis vegetable patch.

4 - To have fun

Gardening is, above all, a pleasure. Touching the ground, watering or even flowering plants and growing fruit is incomparable. In addition, gardening has a beneficial effect on mental health because it generates well-being linked to outdoor activity.

5- Cultivating diversity

The old varieties are rare in supermarkets, so take the opportunity to grow them in your garden! Also, by cultivating your vegetable garden, you will harvest the right vegetable at the right time, and not all at the same time, a pleasure to rediscover! And why not cultivate original vegetable plants to surprise your friends? Discover our exceptional selection!

6- Stimulate Your Creativity

Gardening is a rewarding personal creation. Acting on its surroundings to beautify it and see the result from day to day and from season to season, provides great satisfaction and stimulates creativity.

7 - For the aesthetic aspect

Greening our cities and cultivating our land means improving our living environment while taking advantage of unused spaces. Terraces, roofs and parking lots are all areas of experimentation for urban vegetable gardens! Also, the presence of greenery in our daily environment considerably improves our well-being! Even in the office, green plants improve our productivity!

8 - Learn from nature

How do our foods grow? Essential for children, like adults. The garden is a real school. So if you want to learn, you have to practice. You will take the opportunity to teach your children a lot of your knowledge about insects and vegetables. If your child participates in the vegetable garden, you will no longer hear "I don't like" at mealtime!

9 - Become aware of ecological issues

Learn to recycle, save water in the garden, grow vegetables and discover that hybrid varieties (non-reproducible) are a great scam that is increasingly fattening large multinationals, learn why agriculture has lost its diversity ... yes, all of this awareness of ecological issues and problems.

10 - It benefits biodiversity

By gardening in harmony with nature and without using pesticides, the positive consequences will be great in relation to biodiversity. Your green corner will be a haven of peace for pollinating insects and butterflies. This is all the more important in urban areas, where green areas are sometimes very little present!

As you can see, there's no lack of reasons for growing your own vegetables, so what do you expect? It's time to start gardening and draft your plan for next season's vegetable garden! If your vegetable patch is already growing your own vegetables, what are the reasons for that? Is it just a matter of culture, enjoyment. Perhaps just to find out what you've got on your platter?

Vegetables to grow in your home garden

Cultivating the vegetable garden on the balcony or in the home garden is stimulating and fun, and nowadays also trendy. It makes you earn health, joy, and why not, even in your wallet. Even for those who don't have too much space, we have seen that there are various do-it-yourself vertical garden solutions and just use a little trick to transform your terrace into a splendid urban garden. But what to cultivate? Here, in our opinion, the easy vegetables that are easy to grow, even for those who are beginners with gardening techniques.

Tomatoes (Lycopersicon esculentum)

The tomato is a creeping plant, and for this reason, most varieties must install support. It is rich in nutrients such as, potassium, phosphorus, niacin, antioxidant substances such as lycopene, carotene, anthocyanins, and vitamins A, C, and E. In addition, thanks to their juicy pulp, tomatoes can add a load of taste and flavor to various dishes, such as salads, pasta, and sandwiches.

Prefer a place in your garden with good exposure to sunlight after the winter with its frosts and make sure the acidity of the soil is between six and seven pH. (Add lime to increase the pH level, instead add sulfur to decrease.) Get some good compost (or better yet do it yourself) and mix it with the soil. Dig a hole for each seed, separating it from each other about thirty centimeters to allow the plants to expand, cover it, and slightly press the soil. Water with the aid of a spray bottle several times a week.

Radishes (Raphanus sativus)

Originating in the Chinese and Japanese areas, it is mainly grown for its roots, the edible portion which can be of different colors (red, white, green, purple), shapes and height. Radishes are a great resource of potassium, folic acid, magnesium, and calcium, and are widely used as a seasoning as well as a basic garnish in salads.

Radish is an annual plant, with a very rapid cycle of production. The best time for outdoor sowing is from April to July and, to grow, they need a very sunny soil with a pH of six or seven. They can be planted in broadcasters or rows. The seeds have to be buried a few centimeters below the surface, being careful to leave ample space between them to allow good plant growth. They do not need abundant but regular watering, for they do not bear drought.

Zucchini (Cucurbita pepo)

Apparent to a cucumber, this elongated vegetable made its debut in Italy around 1800. It has a low-calorie content with its characteristic green color and is rich in potassium, folic acid and manganese. Zucchini can be boiled, fried, steamed or cooked in the sun as suggested by us. They could be an excellent side dish, a delicious filling or a delicious appetizer.

Sowing will take place between March and May, by placing two or three seeds on each hole. Depending on the variety we'll pick, the holes will be more or less wide. The dimensions for the winter ones will be 50x50x50, while a hole of 30x30x30 will be sufficient for the summer variety. The holes must be lined with compost and spaced at least one meter. The seeds are to be covered by a twenty-centimeter layer of soil. Water generously every day, and in a few weeks, you will see your seedlings sprout.

Beetroot (Beta vulgaris)

Beetroot is a biennial cycle plant with a fleshy root which can be boiled or eaten alone or in a salad. Betaine is considered to boost the health of the cardiovascular system as one of the key nutrients in this strong red or purple crop.

The first thing to do is clean and strengthen the seeds by immersing them in the water at room temperature for a day. By removing any stones, we prepare the ground and plant the seeds individually by spacing them apart. So water them at least once a day.

Carrots (Daucus carota)

The species is native to temperate regions of Europe and is rich in vitamins A (Betacarotene), B, C, D, E and PP, as well as mineral salts and starches, antioxidants and dietary fibers, of distinctive orange color. Carrots are a delicious and healthy snack, which is an excellent ingredient for cakes to be steamed, baked or boiled.

The sowing can be done according to the varieties from January to October, and it is advisable to do so every 15-25 days in a scalar manner to obtain roots of different sizes. The holes are spaced apart and are to host a few seeds each.

The soil must always be well moist, and the quantity of water will decrease as plants mature.

Spinach (Spinacia oleracea)

Originally from south-western Asia, spinach, was introduced to Europe about 1000, but only during the nineteenth century, it became increasingly popular as food. This plant's dense green leaves are eaten up, very high in iron and calcium.

Prepare the soil for sowing with compost and bury the seeds a few centimeters deep, holding the right distances to allow the plants to grow properly. Water is ample.

Peas (Pisum sativum)

Originally from the Mediterranean and near-eastern area, the pea is an annual herbaceous plant of the Fabaceae family and rich in vitamins A, B, and C.

Mix the soil with nutrient-rich compost, and remember that it will need abundant watering to make peas flourish. Distribute the seeds a few centimeters apart and plant them to a depth of four-five centimeters.

Peppers (Capsicum annuum)

The pepper is an annual Mediterranean herb and a seasonal climate in the warm countries of South America from which it comes. It is rich in vitamins and nutrients such as thiamine, folic acid and manganese and can be used and seasoned in different ways, both cooked and raw.

Fertilize the soil with both compost and Epsom salts, thereby making it more magnesium-rich to make the peppers grow healthier. They bury the surface seeds since they grow best in warm soils. Water periodically, keeping the soil moist.

Otherwise, it can get a bitter taste after you harvest your peppers.

Lettuce (Lactuca Sativa)

It is an annual plant with more or less large, ovoid or elongated leaves and it has different shades of color depending on the variety, ranging from green to yellowish to red.

It was considered an aphrodisiac in ancient Egypt. Lettuce is a good source of folic acid and vitamin A. Used as the main ingredient in most salads, and this green leafy vegetable can also be stuffed with different ingredients, of which there are dozens of popular varieties.

Before cultivating the soil, fertilize it with nutrients and work it by removing any stones or debris. Make sure the seeds are planted at a depth of between eight and sixteen centimeters and water every morning.

Onion (Allium cepa)

The first signs date back to the Bronze Age. It is a herbaceous biennial plant with a collated root system, rich in fiber, folic acid and vitamin C These bulb vegetables add flavor to a large variety of food items, including sauces, soups, salads and more.

To allow the bulb to grow homogeneously, the soil must be very light, and for this, it must be worked vigorously and free from debris. It is enriched with compost. Plant the seeds a few centimeters deep and well-spaced apart. And this sector is often but gentle and every week provides them with about an inch of water.

CHAPTER NINE

Types of Fertilizer for your garden

You will be faced with the need for fertilizer some time in your gardening, whether you cultivate vegetables or flowers. Nevertheless, many of the commercially available fertilizers are produced from chemical processes that are harmful to the environment. Natural alternatives are available, which will keep your gardens, family and earth safe.

Some of the best things you can do to feed your plants for your garden is not to pick the grass clippings. Let the clippings remain on the grass, instead of using a catcher on your mower. They'll decompose easily and bring essential nutrients back to your lawn. Fast, simple, and free-natural fertilization do not get much better.

Find seaweed, either gathered on its own or bought in the liquid extract from your garden center, for your vegetable and flower beds. This diamond is filled with minerals and trace elements; besides, if worked into the whole soil, its composition tends to help hold the plant's moisture. Most gardeners say this is the only fertilizer you'll ever have to use, and it's completely chemical-free.

When you have access to animal manure, consider using it; it's full of the nitrogen which your plants need. It's better to use rotted down manure, however, because fresh manure will burn the roots of your plants. All kinds of organic manure can be bought, from sheep and cows to the more exotic bat guano. Once it's worked into the soil, it's not nearly as smelly as you might think.

Many natural fertilizers that enjoy large use are blood and bone meal, beer (yep, beer), and coffee grounds.

Nonetheless, make sure that your soil is tested before adding something. You do not have to add something or add just one or two things, such as lime. You can't add anything. More is not better in fertilizer matters, and most plants can do well with a wise eye. You will assist with the soil check and the definition of your local county extension office so that you know exactly what you're dealing with. When you are dealing with your garden, it is always better to be safe than sorry!

Nutrient requirements of garden plants

Plants mainly need macronutrients, i.e., nitrogen, phosphorus and potassium:

1. Nitrogen (chemical symbol N). It contributes to the development of foliage and stems or branches. It is an important fertilizer in the spring when the vegetation is recovering. But beware, used in excess, not only

pollutes the water and the soil, but it unbalances the plants, which then produce more leaves at the expense of flowers and fruits. The most nitrogen-intensive plants are grass, grasses, bamboo and leafy vegetables.

2. Phosphorus (chemical symbol P). It contributes to the development of the roots, and it strengthens the resistance of plants in the face of diseases. Used in excess, it contributes to the eutrophication of water (that is to say, the proliferation of algae). The most demanding plants in phosphorus are flowering and fruiting species, as well as seed vegetables.

3. Potassium (chemical symbol K). It contributes to flowering and fruit development. The most demanding plants in potassium are fruit trees, flowering shrubs, roses, bulbs and root vegetables.

In variable proportions, the fertilizer can only have 1 or 2 elements or blends 3. Numbers showing the exact composition are accompanied by the initials of NPK. The fertilizer containing 16% nitrogen (N), 5% phosphorus (P) and 5% potassium (K) for example NKP 16-5-5 shows.

Plants need secondary nutrients in a lesser extent, such as calcium (C), sulfur (S) and magnesium (Mg), as well as trace elements, such as Iron (Fe), manganese (Mn), copper (Cu), zinc (Zn), silicon (Si), and more. But secondary nutrients are normally present in adequate amounts unless there is a soil deficiency or according to its PH. It is best for your soil to be tested before any fertilizer supply to learn its strengths and imbalances.

The different types of fertilizers

Macronutrients, secondary nutrients, and trace elements come from different sources. Thus nitrogen is present in dried blood, which is an organic fertilizer and in nettle manure, which is considered as an ecological fertilizer. Phosphorus comes from phosphate rock, so it is a mineral fertilizer, but it is also found in bone powder, which is an organic fertilizer. The same is true for potassium. Without forgetting that N, P, and K can also come from the chemical industry... It is, therefore, not by their composition that we can recognize this or that type of fertilizer but rather by their manufacture or their origin.

- Chemical fertilizers: These are synthetic products made from chemical elements.
- L are organic fertilizers: They are of animal origin (Powder bones or fish bones, dried blood, crushed horn, guano) or vegetable (algae, nettle manure or comfrey, ash, the residue of vinasse sugar beet, etc.).
- Mineral fertilizers: They come from natural deposits of inert minerals such as potash or phosphate. But most of the time, they are actually made from chemical elements.

- Ecological or natural fertilizers: These are natural mineral fertilizers, organic fertilizers when they come from natural plant or animal materials. Nettle, comfrey purines are considered ecological fertilizers.
- Green manures: These are fast-growing plants (clover, alfalfa, lupine, horse bean, etc.), which are sown and buried on-site to provide a natural fertilizer rich in organic matter. In the garden, before installing a lawn, it is a good way to fertilize the soil.

CHAPTER TEN

Pests, prevention and treatment

Most Common Pests In Your Garden

Insects are always present in our garden. Many times we think that all can harm our plants, but that is not true. Learn about the most common pest insects in the garden, their characteristics and what you can do to control them.

Aphids

Aphids are a tiny fly, measuring 0.9-3 mm. There are over 4,000 species, but some 250 are considered pests. Its color may be gray, white, red or black, and there are wings in some species. Its mouth apparatus is a sucker, meaning it feeds on the plant's sap. We can find plenty of vegetables, like lettuce, tomato, eggplant, cauliflower, spinach, chili, kale, etc. Aphids transmit diseases, so monitoring our plants is very important. We can find them at the leaves and growth points on the underside.

7 Red Aphids

To cool them we can add water on the underside of the plants with biodegradable soap, do it really early in the morning or in the afternoon when the sun does not touch the plants anymore. Some natural enemies of aphids are parasitic wasps (Aphelinus abdominals, Aphidius colemani, Aphidius ervi), Catarina (Coccinellidae), lacewing (Chrysoperla carnea), parasitic fly (Apidoletes sp)

Larvae or caterpillars

There are various forms of larvae in our garden; various sizes and colors. But what exactly is a larva? Larvae are the juvenile stage of some metamorphosis-bearing insects. The larvae which affect our plants come from butterflies or moths of the night.

8 - Larvae or caterpillar

The larvae can be 1-7 cm in size and can have a black, white, gray, brown color. The larvae are insect chewing and can be located on the underside of the leaves, at the point of growth or in the dirt. They attack most plants in our garden, in this botanical family, in particular broccoli, cauliflower, kale and other plants.

We can use soap and garlic and chili extract with biodegradable water to control them. Apply very early in the morning or evening when the plants no longer receive the sun's rays. It's a simple method even to extract them by hand. Some natural larvae enemies are lacewing (Chrysoperla carnea) and the Bt (Bacillus thuringiensis) bacteria.

Whitefly

9 - Whitefly

The whitefly is a small (1mm) powdery white insect. This fly feeds on the sap of the plant, reducing its productivity. A side effect of whitefly is disease transmission. We find it on the underside of the leaves of many plants such as; tomatoes, aubergines, pumpkin, cucumber, flowers such as poinsettia and jamaica, among others. Some natural enemies are the Catarina, lacewing, predatory beetles (Orius sp), parasitic wasps (Encarsia sp). We can also apply soapy water or yellow traps.

Leaf miners

10 - Leaf miners

The leaf miner is a tiny larva that we can find in the leaves of our plants. They make small galleries or paths between the leaves, taking away space for the plant to carry out its photosynthesis. The most effective control is to locate the larva on the leaf and crush it with our fingers, making sure that you do not hurt the plant.

Chapulines

The chapulines are a common pest that can cause a lot of damage since they eat the leaves and, in some cases, the whole plant. These insects can eat any plant. The grasshoppers can be up to 8cm long. For the control of grasshoppers, we can count on spiders, mantises, Bacillus thuringiensis (Bt, bacteria) and Beauveria bassiana (fungus).

Red spider

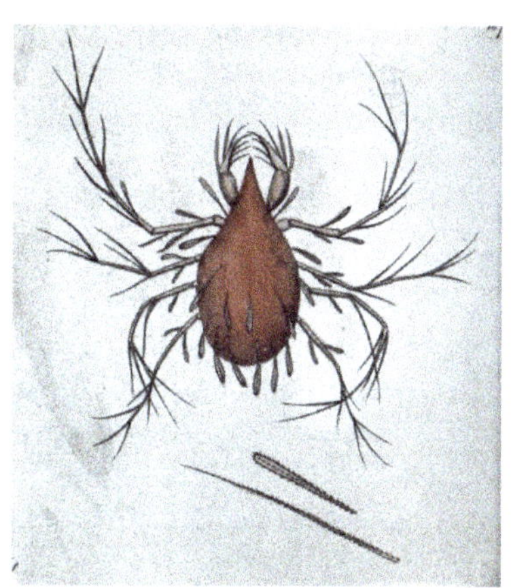

11 - Red Spider[1]

The red spider is a very small insect (0.5mm) that feeds on the sap of plants. Always in a group. These insects form a white spider web on the leaves and stems, thereby protecting themselves from predators. They can attack strawberry,

---

[1] Credit: https://wellcomecollection.org/works/wmcg49n3

eggplant, squash, tomato, corn, chili, melon, potato, and trees. For its control, an extract of garlic and chili can be applied. If the plant is severely affected, it is best to remove it to avoid spreading to other plants. Good prevention is crop rotation.

Trips

Thrips are small insects that measure between 1-3mm. It is a yellowish-brown or brown color. They feed on the sap of the plant, and they can cause leaf spots and transmit diseases. These insects are attracted to the blue color, and you can put a blue container with water and some soap or sticky traps. Thrips have several natural predators, such as some varieties of mites and the Orius bug (Orius sp).

Mealybugs

Mealybugs are small (6mm) black or grayish in color. They feed on the leaves and stems of plants. Very common behavior in mealybugs is that they curl up to protect themselves, forming a small ball. If our soil is well nourished, it will not be a problem for our garden.

Snails and slugs

Snails and slugs are mollusks that live in humid areas and water reservoirs. They feed on all kinds of plants and can end up destroying the entire garden. We can identify the damage by the traces of mucus that they leave behind. We can prevent the arrival of snails by having our plants in elevated places and using aromatic herbs. Remember they are looking for cool and humid places. For its control, we can use coffee beans, beer traps or eggshells.

Nematodes

Nematodes are small plant parasites found in the soil. Its shape is like an earthworm, and they measure between 0.2-1mm depending on the species. These small individuals feed on the roots of the plants, but there are species that are beneficial (they are biological control for some insects). To control the nematodes in the soil, we can plant garlic cloves, and this will serve as a repellent. It is also important to have a crop rotation and fertilize our soil.

You can find many pests in your garden, but controlling them is not that difficult. Remember to check your garden frequently, once or twice a week. Look well under the leaves, and there you can find many pests and other insects.

Vegetable Gardening Problems – Prevention

There are many alternatives to synthetic insecticides to control some unwanted insects that we commonly call as garden pests. It is first important to know which insects are harmful to plants and which are beneficial, the natural allies of the garden. These allies are very important in preventing pests and diseases as they help to protect the plants against some hungry insects that appear more frequently in the spring. There are still other good practices that must be considered in pest prevention!

How to prevent pests in an organic garden

1. Choose the vegetable varieties most resistant to insects and diseases. Whenever possible, we should choose seeds from organic or biodynamic agriculture. In addition, it is preferable to produce seedlings for transplanting.

2. Provide shelter for natural enemies of pests, such as predatory insects (spiders, ladybugs), bats, birds.

3. Improve the soil structure, adding organic compost or making green manure. As a result, healthy soil will allow healthier plants to grow.

4. Grow aromatic and medicinal herbs to bring beneficial insects to the garden. In addition, some have a repellent effect on pests.

5. Try to plant in a small space in order to see if there is damage caused by any present pest. In this way, we understand if there is already a pest installed, and should apply home remedies to control.

6. Cut the first infected plants and remove them from the site. So, by removing the residues from the infected crops, we will help to interrupt the insect's biological cycles.

7. Take into account the practices of favorable intercropping of cultures. Consequently, this practice also helps to benefit from more effective management of soil space and nutrients.

8. Always use natural preventive methods, such as biological control. Furthermore, we must collect the pests manually when they are easily visible.

9. Avoid monocultures in beds or plots with an area greater than 1 m2. As a result, we promote greater biodiversity, cultivating, for example, some flowering plants such as marigolds, chamomile, capucinhas, among others.

10. Promote crop rotation. Above all, don't grow the same types of vegetables in the same place every year. We can do a 3-year rotation in 3 sites or a 4-year rotation in 4 plots (more advisable).

Many pests swarm in gardens and attack all plants, whether vegetables, fruit trees or even ornamental plants. Discover how to treat a garden against pests depending on the species you face.

Treat a garden against mealybug

Scale insects generally proliferate on fruit trees from which they suck the sap, causing sores and proliferation of fungi.

To remove them, the use of solutions based on methylated spirits and black soap is necessary—softer treatment but just as effective: ladybugs, deadly enemies of cochineal.

Fight against aphids

Aphids also suck the sap from plants, slowing their growth. Vectors of viruses and fungi, they readily settle on roses and fruit trees.

Here again, the ladybug can help get rid of the pest, just like nettle manure and repellents (lavender, thyme, mint ...).

Treat plants against snails and slugs

Snails and slugs appreciate the sap of plants and devour their leaves, bulbs, fruits and roots.

The "ramparts" of ash and wood chips installed around the plantations help to slow down these pests. To remove them, there are chemicals based on iron phosphate.

Protect a garden from mites

Some mites (including the red spider) suck the sap from the trees, resulting in desiccation and discoloration of the leaves.

The first bulwark against mites: humidity. Watering the plants well is, therefore, essential. In the case of invasion, there are acaricides, but one can also use the "services" of their predator, Phytoseiulus persimilis.

Treatment against moths

The larvae of the moth (moth) feed on many plants. Leaves, stems, fruits, buds ... are ingested.

Preventive methods to limit egg-laying are essential here: suppress weeds, hoeing, mulching, watering ... If necessary, we will use a phytosanitary product or the Thuringian bacillus (caterpillar killer bacteria).

Treat fruit worm

The codling moth (fruit worm) is a caterpillar that feeds mainly on the flesh of fruits.

To prevent its appearance, there are pheromone traps that limit its fertilization. If necessary, we will spray bacterospeine (natural insecticide) on the affected tree. One can also enshrine spared fruits and destroy those infected.

CONCLUSION

You have many options to escape from the non-productive or poorly grown garden, one of which is how to integrate the advantage of having one or two raised beds in your backyard. We've concluded that a raised bed has advantages over the ordinary bed as you control the soil you are using, and you can garden in a more comfortable location. In addition, the different soil conditions needed for individual plants can be managed more efficiently and can be varied from bed to bed.

A pH soil test kit helps have the right conditions for individual plants. You will quickly get loose, well-drained soil because you do not walk to compact it. Raised garden beds drain much better off surface water, good news for areas with heavy soils and high rainfall than normal garden beds. This will help the plants trap air across the root system, which is a big plus for warm, stable plants.

You should tend your elevated garden bed in a comfortable position to help protect against backaches that can often stop you from trying to supply fresh quality produce for the family. It is also better for people with disabilities or who have to take a seat in the garden. We agree that raised gardens are a great help to any gardener.

There is a range of materials and sizes to choose from when determining whether to create your own garden beds. The availability of space defines the size and number of beds. You can buy kits or build your own from anything that holds dirt, such as wood, plastic, bricks, or rocks, very easily. Lumber is the most used and probably the easiest to use.

When planning the raised bed, there are certain things to think about. First, decide on a comfortable height for you to maintain your plants from any angle without having to walk on the elevated gardens, thus preventing the soil from getting compact. The raised bed should be placed in a position where the plants you want to grow to have a ray of sufficient sunshine, which leaves enough room for wheelbarrows and other tools. In order to address any issues with drainage, elevated gardens should be a minimum of 6 inches in height; it is also prudent to cover the area in order to avoid ruin and soil erosion.

Usually, you just take over the entire dimensions into your garden center when building raised gardens, and they will work out what you need. When you know in advance what plants should be used for your raised garden, it will advise and provide the correct soil mix. We advise you to fill the beds with a half organic matter and a half soil if you raise the beds only up to 15 inches. Know that composting your own reduces your total costs.

Now, if you look at large, three-foot, raised gardens, it is fair that you take a different course of action to produce good results and seek to reduce costs. You may half fill it with rocks or sand to minimize the amount of soil required to fill this vast area, then fill it with a 50-50 mixture of manure or compost and soil. Adjust the pH levels for your plants, and this will give your elevated garden the ultimate conditions for growth.

www.ingramcontent.com/pod-product-compliance
Lightning Source LLC
Chambersburg PA
CBHW071606030726
47593CB00001BA/341